The Complete Conjuring Spirits

A Manual of Modern Sorcery

MICHAEL OSIRIS SNUFFIN

2020

First printing, 2020
Throned Eye Press

ISBN: 9798625917827

Dedication

To three great seers...
Mary, Leo, and Sam

...and four magical uncles
Uncle Al, Uncle Izzy,
Uncle Anton, and Uncle Pete.

I could not have accomplished
this without you.

Thank you.

TABLE OF CONTENTS

CHAPTER ONE

The Mechanics of Sorcery

This manual provides basic instructions for performing effective evocations of spiritual entities. But before we get into the practical work of sorcery, I want to give you some theory to put our work into perspective. Let's examine how the spirit world works, how it affects us, and how we interact with it.

A GENERAL THEORY OF SORCERY

Two planes of existence comprise the Universe. On the Material plane, the Universe manifests primarily as matter, the world perceived by the five senses, described as natural, solid, and objective. On the Etheric plane, the Universe manifests primarily as energy, usually beyond the normal perception of the five senses and described as supernatural, fluid, and subjective. These two planes coexist, with matter on the Material plane intimately linked to its energetic counterpart on the Etheric plane.

Changes in one plane of existence lead to changes in the other plane, but the fluidic and subjective energy of the Etheric plane often proves easier to manipulate than the solid and objective matter of the Material plane. Magick causes change to occur on the Material plane through the manipulation of the Etheric plane in conformity with will. Standard ceremonial magick on the Material plane transforms your will into energy and launches it into the Etheric plane to do its work. Sorcery involves contacting spirits that live on the Etheric plane and asking them to do the work for you in exchange for energy.

While an infinite number of spirits inhabit the Etheric plane, sorcerers do not work with all of them. To understand why, we must examine the basic differences between the entities of the Etheric plane.

THE SPIRITUAL CONTINUUM

Our Judeo-Christian culture conditions us to look at the Universe in terms of dualities such as black/white, light/dark, and good/evil, and this bias also colors our common perception of the spirit world. We may more accurately express the differences between spiritual entities inhabiting the Etheric plane within a continuum primarily based on their complexity:

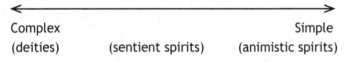

Complex		Simple
(deities)	(sentient spirits)	(animistic spirits)

The most complex spirits manifest as deities, goddesses and gods of myth with divine powers. Animism gives all Material parts a corresponding spirit; thus the smallest bits of matter such as grains of sand and drops of water will also have spirits attached to them, entities called animistic spirits. Sentient spirits inhabit the vast realm between the two extremes, and include Elementals, angels, planetary spirits, demonic spirits, and many others.

Spirit   Matter

Another defining characteristic of spirits within the continuum concerns their relationship to matter. The most complex spirits have independent spiritual identities on the Etheric plane, while animistic spirits have strong bonds to their Material plane counterparts. For example, Poseidon has many attributes and myths that define him and describe his great power over water on the two planes; the spirit of a drop of water has no identity, its actions primarily determined by forces on the Material plane.

Active Belief   Passive Belief

The last characteristic to consider has to do with the nature of belief in the spirits, for belief provides them with a source of energy. Deities receive their power from the active belief of people on the Material plane and the lesser spirits of the Etheric plane. The empowerment of animistic spirits comes primarily from passive belief in their Material characteristics. We actively believe in Poseidon by building temples, performing rituals, and offering prayers in his name; we passively believe in water, its properties and uses, and in its vital ability to sustain life.

The sentient spirits that sorcerers seek to communicate with reside in the middle of these three continuums, but special rules apply to the spirits near the each end, so we'll talk about them first.

Deities inhabit the complex end of the continuum, the gods and goddesses of spiritual pantheons. They have complex, multifaceted personalities and possess extraordinary abilities.

Deities have a great deal of control over energies and entities on the Etheric plane, and have the potential to cause large changes on the Material plane by orchestrating them on the Etheric plane.

As mentioned before, deities receive much of their power from their believers and servants, corporeal or otherwise. Belief equals energy, so the more people that believe in a deity, the more power it has at its disposal. Because of their powerful nature, we cannot evoke deities using the methods of sorcery; interaction with deities requires some form of theurgy.

The smallest animistic spirits amass on the simple end of the continuum: the spirits of grains, whispers, drops, sparks, rays, and thoughts that form the building blocks of every Elemental and spirit. Individually, they have little power; but when collected and combined into more cognizant, cohesive entities, they develop into sentient spirits, the spirits of the Elements, the spirits of everything. Animistic spirits may even combine to form deities; modern examples include James Lovelock's Gaia hypothesis and Peter Carroll's conception of Baphomet.[1]

Beyond a certain scale, spirits lack the cohesion and coherency to interact with them in a meaningful way. Thus the Ancient Greeks didn't invent spirits for individual drops of water, but when the water collected in pools, springs, and streams, they discovered Nereids, Naiads, and Undines. Qabalistic magicians frequently evoke the Choirs of Angels when working the Archangels of the sephiroth, but I have yet to discover a Qabalist crazy enough to identify and evoke individual Angels from the multitude that make up the Angelic Choirs.

---

1   James Lovelock, *The Ages of Gaia*. rev.ed. (New York: W.W. Norton, 1995); Peter J. Carroll, *Liber Null & Psychonaut* (York Beach, ME: Samuel Weiser, 1987), 156-161.

OBJECTIVE IDENTITY

As all Material phenomena have an Etheric counterpart, all sentient spirits also have a Material basis. The term objective identity describes the existence of sentient spirits on the Material plane as expressed through thought, word, or deed. The objective identity of a sentient spirit determines the general nature of the spirit; the subjective identity develops with personal experience.

A practically infinite number of sentient spirits inhabit the Etheric plane. However, three particular types of spirits have received the most attention in Western Esotericism: angelic spirits, demonic spirits,[2] and Enochian (Watchtower) entities. The basis of our relationship with these spirits depends on the strength of their objective identity.

Angelic spirits have a strong objective identity. They have played a prominent role in Judeo-Christian culture as messengers, protectors, punishers, and healers. Most people in Western culture know what angels look like, even people that do not believe in them; we find angels not only in Biblical and apocryphal texts, but also in art and literature.

Archangels administrate the rest of the angelic spirits. Of all the angels, only the Archangels possess names, well-defined characteristics, and specific abilities. Hermetic Qabalists assigned the most popular Archangels to sephiroth of the Tree of Life and also gave them Elemental, Planetary and Zodiacal attributions.

This high level of definition gives the Archangels a very strong objective identity. They generally appear as beautiful, fair-skinned, androgynous people who radiate divine light. They possess great wisdom and kindness, and have an innate desire to help humanity heal and perfect itself. One knows what to expect

---

2   In the Judeo-Christian paradigm, "demonic" often meant "not Christian." Thus, not all of the spirits labeled as demons appear and act like mythical demons.

when working with Archangels.

Goetic and other so-called demonic spirits have a weaker objective identity than the Archangels. The *Goetia* gives us a physical description of each spirit followed by a list of services it performs. However, experience shows that the actual appearance of Goetic spirits varies considerably from the descriptions, and that these spirits have many abilities beyond those described in the grimoire.

Furthermore, sorcerers have very different experiences and relationships with the same Goetic spirit as they discover its subjective identity. One sorcerer may find the spirit friendly; another may struggle to get the spirit to do anything more than make condescending remarks. Not all will find Orobas agreeable, and Bael does not always act like the nasty demon of Christian mythology.

The challenge of working with Enochian spirits comes from the fact that they have almost no objective identity. They possess no real attributes other than their Elemental nature and have no well-defined abilities or powers. As a result, sorcerers' accounts of their highly subjective experiences with Enochian spirits often have little in common.

Enochian entities may appear and act in a strange or even alien manner, and they seem to have difficulty understanding how the Material plane works, especially when you talk to entities further down in the hierarchy. It appears that their lack of objective identity inhibits their ability to comprehend concepts on the Material plane.

THE POWER OF NAMES AND SIGILS

Naming something gives you power over it. The names of spirits form the basis of their objective identity; by identifying a spirit, you can interact with it. The Ancient Egyptians understood the power of names very well; the Egyptian books of the dead document a journey through the strange landscape of the afterlife, where you must properly address the gods in order to speak with them, correctly name gates to pass through them, and even identify objects to use them.

The name of a spirit must possess enough definition to correctly identify it, and sometimes you may require additional names and titles to fully define whom you seek to evoke. Run around a crowded public place yelling "Michael! Michael!" and more than a couple of heads will likely turn your way; yet none of them will answer to my full name. Likewise, when a conjurer I once seered for called out, "I do evoke thee, Michael! Come forth and speak with me!" the Archangel Michael did not show up. The entity that appeared looked like an angel taken from the cover art of a 60's psychedelic rock album. The conjurer quickly banished "Michael"—who didn't have much to say anyway—and then specifically called forth the desired Archangel Michael.

Traditionally, names have the most power when written or spoken in their original languages. Exceptions arise when variants or more popular names predominate; to the common man the name Jesus has more power than the Hebrew Yeheshuah, and the Greek name Osiris more power than the Egyptian Asar. However, few significant exceptions occur below the level of divinity.

The true name of a spirit serves as an essential tool for verification of its identity. Vibrating the name of a spirit strengthens it, just as vibrating the name of another spirit or force counter to its nature will weaken the spirit. If you demand that spirits state and sign their true names, they usually comply.

You can also use names to establish authority over a spirit. In the Enochian and Qabalistic hierarchies, naming spiritual superiors in the conjuration compels the spirit to appear and obey. The Judeo-Christian paradigm demonized many of the spirits of ancient cultures, so grimoires often use the names of Jehovah and his minions to compel spirits. If you do not work within the Christian paradigm and the names of Jehovah do not move you, do not use these pre-packaged conjurations. Write your own instead, as conjurations energized by the power of personal beliefs will have much more power.

Sigils create patterns of force on the Etheric plane that constrain and harness specific energies. Sigils represent a non-verbal Material link to Etheric inhabitants. However, simply drawing a sigil does not make it work; otherwise just opening a book like the *Goetia* to the wrong page could have disastrous results. Activating a sigil on the Etheric plane makes a sigil function. The difference between a drawn sigil and activated sigil reflects the objective and subjective aspects of the spirit.

The activation of sigils happens in one of two ways: formal consecration or use in evocation. Consecration involves performing a short ritual to magically link the spirit with the sigil. Using the sigil in a successful evocation will also activate it, as the operation links the spirit with the sigil.

Others who gaze upon your activated sigils may accidentally and unconsciously form a link with the spirits they belong to, so you must keep your sigils away from prying eyes. The risk of accidental linkage increases with sigils of demonic entities, which seem to enjoy finding new avenues of exploration and experience, often to the detriment of those who cannot readily perceive or control them.

Names and sigils form the core of practical grimoires, which function as phone books for the inhabitants of the Etheric plane. If you can't find a sigil to copy out of a book, you can always make your own. I use the Word method given in Peter Carroll's *Liber Null* to sigilize spirit names.[3] *Liber Null* also gives instructions on how to create your own spirits (servitors), if so desired.

If names truly have more power when spoken and written in their original languages, it follows that sigils will have more power when created from the letters or characters of their native languages. With this idea in mind, we can address a curious omission in the Enochian system, where only the Elemental Kings have sigils. Using the word method in conjunction with the Enochian alphabet will create strange but effective sigils for rest of the entities in the Enochian system.

MOTIVES FOR EVOCATION

Why do people work with spirits? Motives vary among sorcerers.

In general, most sorcerers work with spirits to get assistance with their personal and spiritual development. Archangels and Angelic spirits devote themselves to helping people develop and evolve. Enochian entities and other Elemental spirits show interest in helping magicians achieve Elemental balance. Working with demonic spirits often involves taking control of disruptive spirits working against you and convincing them to work with you for

---

3   Carroll, *Liber Null & Psychonaut*, 20-22.

mutual benefit instead.

Spirits also benefit from sorcerous relationships. By working with the spirits, you help them strengthen their objective identities, which in turn helps them to grow and evolve. Most demonic spirits seem to have an objective identity crisis, which explains why they often demand so much attention and usually crave material rewards.

Other magicians get involved in sorcery to satisfy an innate curiosity, a desire for exploration, and a thirst for knowledge. Humanity has always had a keen interest in the Etheric plane and its inhabitants. Sorcery allows us to experience and interact with the normally hidden Etheric world that we live in. It also helps us gain an understanding of how the Etheric plane functions and affects our lives.

This instinct for Etheric exploration has led many people to work with the Enochian system. In the twentieth century, the published rituals of the Golden Dawn revealed the great power of Enochian entities to a much broader audience. Experiences with the most accessible rituals (like the Opening by Watchtower) compelled many magicians to investigate the Enochian system in greater depth. The fact that these entities have almost no objective identity only seems to increase our interest in them.

Magicians also have practical reasons for using evocation instead of other forms of magick. The primary benefit comes from the fact that we can engage in complex interactions with spirits. Spirits can follow detailed instructions and complete complicated tasks that prove more difficult to accomplish using other methods of ceremonial magick. Spirits generally adapt better than spells to the unpredictable and chaotic situations encountered in modern urban life.

Sorcery also gives you a greater deal of control over your magical operations. If you change your mind about an operation and wish to end it, call up the spirit, tell it to stop, and give it something else to do. If an operation fails, you can call up the spirit to find out what went wrong as well as what needs to change to get things right. You may then instruct the spirit to work on its task until completed, or summon up another spirit to do the job.

Now that we have established a spiritual paradigm for the basic mechanics of sorcery, we have a basis to understand the practical work that follows.

CHAPTER TWO

Archangelic Evocation

I always encourage aspiring sorcerers to begin with the evocation of the Qabalistic Archangels. These beneficent entities possess great patience and wisdom, and as a rule, they do not lie. Their benign nature allows the neophyte to practice the art of evocation without fear or pressure. When the sorcerer feels comfortable with the mechanics of evocation, they may move on to working with more challenging spirits, such as those from the *Goetia*.

I also recommend Archangelic work for neophytes because many magicians take up the Lesser Banishing Ritual of the Pentagram (LBRP) as their first circle creation ritual, and the LBRP employs the Archangels of the Elements. By calling each Archangel up, introducing yourself, and conversing with them, you can form a powerful bond with them that will extend beyond the evocation. After you speak to Raphael, Gabriel, Michael and Auriel, they manifest with much more power when invoked in the LBRP.

The method of evocation described in Part Three: Practical Goetic Magick works for most spirits found in Western Esotericism, including the Archangels. Only the format of the conjuration differs, as you have to identify the attributes of the Archangel you wish to summon. The conjuration has to specify what sphere or Element the Archangel governs, and includes a Hebrew god-name to empower and summon the Archangel:

"I do evoke thee, O [Name], Archangel of [Attribution], in the name of [god-name] to manifest in the Triangle before me, that I may converse with thee and employ thy services."

For example:

"I do evoke thee, O Raphael, Archangel of Tiphareth, in the name of YHVH Eloah v'Daath to manifest in the Triangle before me, that I may converse with thee and employ thy services."

If you wish, you may embellish the conjuration by naming additional characteristics of the Archangel and including more Hebrew god-names. In my first evocations, I added the god-names from the LBRP (YHVH, Eheieh, Adonai, and AGLA) to my conjurations. Daily practice of the LBRP had given these god-names more meaning and power than the designated Sephirotic and Planetary god-names at that time.

Archangels of the Elements

Element	Archangel	God-name
Fire	Michael	AGLA
Water	Gabriel	Eloah
Air	Raphael	Eheieh
Earth	Auriel	Adonai

Archangels of the Planets

Planet	Archangel	God-name
Sol	Michael	YHVH Eloah v'Daath
Luna	Gabriel	Shaddai El Chai
Mars	Camael	Elohim Gibor
Mercury	Raphael	YHVH Tzabaoth
Jupiter	Sachiel	El
Venus	Anael	Elohim Tzabaoth
Saturn	Cassiel	YHVH Elohim

Archangels of the Tree of Life

Sephira	Archangel	God-name
Kether	Metatron	Eheieh
Chokmah	Ratziel	Ya
Binah	Zaphkiel	YHVH Elohim
Chesed	Zadkiel	El
Geburah	Kamael	Elohim Gibor
Tiphareth	Raphael	YHVH Eloah v'Daath
Hod	Haniel	YHVH Tzabaoth
Netzach	Michael	Elohim Tzabaoth
Yesod	Gabriel	Shaddai El Chai
Malkuth	Sandalphon	Adonai ha-Aretz

I have included tables listing the primary attributions of the most common Archangels and the Hebrew god-names associated with them to assist you in writing your own conjurations. Archangels have a strong objective identity; you can easily find information on their abilities and additional attributions, so I will leave it to you to do more research.

You can find Archangelic sigils in books, or you can make your own using the Word method or the Rose Cross method of the Golden Dawn, which draws them on a glyph designed for sigilizing Hebrew names.[4]

Note that the Archangels Gabriel, Michael, and Raphael each have three different attributions, and thus appear on all three tables. Many Qabalists believe that a separate Archangel governs each attribution, and that each set of Archangels simply shares a common name. My experience shows that each attribution represents different faces or aspects of the same Archangel. Both perspectives work; judge for yourself.

Two of the Sephirotic Archangels, Gabriel and Michael, have special knowledge and abilities that new sorcerers will find useful. The Archangel Gabriel, who rules over both Yesod and Water, gives assistance and advice on developing the ability to skry, or sense phenomena on the Etheric plane. We will cover skrying in more detail in Part Three.

The Archangel Michael gives valuable insight and advice on sorcery. He also serves as a protector, and sorcerers of old inscribed his name within the traditional Triangle of evocation to restrain unruly spirits. If you have any questions or concerns about evoking spirits from the Goetia, the Watchtower System, or any other grimoire, call up the Archangel Michael and ask him for help.

One final note: you do not have to believe in Christianity or practice Qabala to work with Archangels. They find meaning and purpose in helping humanity learn and evolve, and they do not care which religion or spiritual path you follow.

---

4   Konstantinos, *Summoning Spirits* (St. Paul; MN: Llewellyn Publications, 2004), 123-127.

CHAPTER THREE

Practical Goetic Magick

INTRODUCTION

The New Aeon of Magick has fostered a great deal of interest in the art of Goetic evocation. Magicians have published more books on the subject in the last forty years than in any other period in history. In this golden age of information, we have access to everything from the original Sloane manuscripts that comprise the *Goetia* to the Goetic journals of modern magicians.

But as with many occult subjects, the proliferation of information on Goetic evocation has spawned some confusing, misleading, and even erroneous instructions on how to properly and effectively perform an operation. Furthermore, the modern magician has little practical use for the traditional methods of evocation such as those described in the *Goetia* and the *Greater Key of Solomon*, grimoires plagued by unnecessary complexity and archaic baggage.

Yet underneath the complicated preparations and wordy conjurations of the *Goetia* lie simple rules and formulae. This work aspires to evoke the *Goetia* from the dark ages and into a modern light. The methods of sorcery described herein also work for evocation of demonic spirits from other grimoires as well as many other Etheric entities in Western Esotericism. When freed from the fetters of Old Aeon tradition and methodology, evocation becomes a practical and effective method of magical working

DISCLAIMER

Working with Goetic spirits has its perils. History refers to them as demons for a reason. Not all spirits will want to work with you, and some may act rebellious, malicious, and even malevolent toward anyone who dares to disturb them. I've heard of Conjurers that have had spirits turn against them, and rumor has it that a few Goetic magicians have even gone mad after their evocations went awry. From what I have observed, problems with Goetic spirits generally come from two sources.

The primary source of problems stems from incompetence or ignorance on the part of the magician. Do not undertake Goetic evocations without proper preparation! You will need experience and proficiency with ceremonial magick, especially banishing rituals. I also advise you to follow a magical path of personal evolution and enlightenment, as it will help you understand your successes and failures.

Second, some of those who descend into madness as a result of a Goetic evocation appear to lack mental stability in the first place. Magical work in general and Goetic evocation in particular will force you to confront your personal demons, like it or not. Good self-confidence and a sound mind make a good foundation for successful Goetic work.

I will take no responsibility for the results of the misuse or abuse of the information offered here. True magicians take responsibility for their own actions, and those who deny that responsibility soon find themselves overwhelmed by it.

THE OPERATORS

The traditional Goetic evocation requires two operators: a Conjurer and a Seer. The Conjurer calls up, binds, and converses with the spirit, while the Seer receives information from the spirit and relays it to the Conjurer.

You may perform a Goetic evocation with one person acting as both Conjurer and Seer, but the operation gets more complicated when you fly solo. The reason lies with the fact that the Conjurer plays a very active role in evocation, performing the rituals, reciting the conjurations and engaging the spirit in conversation. On the other hand, the Seer plays a very passive role, relaying information in a trance state and ideally affecting the communication between the Conjurer and the spirit as little as possible.

To perform an evocation solo, the sorcerer must switch between the active (Conjurer) and passive (Seer) roles, both evoking and receiving information, a difficult task for the neophyte. Goetic evocation often works better when separate people perform these roles. Ideally, the Conjurer and the Seer should switch roles on occasion. This promotes a more complete understanding of both roles involved and keeps the team from getting into a rut.

Bringing in an independent person (a Seer) who has little or no stake in the outcome of the evocation also helps to short-circuit the Conjurer's lust of result. However, if you decide to bring in an untested Seer, take care in selecting who you work with. Unfortunately, one of the last Seers I worked with lacked the ability to skry effectively. I grew concerned when none of my evocations showed any results, good or bad, and I lost out on a few opportunities. When I stopped working with the young poseur, my evocations suddenly started bearing fruit again, and only then did I realize what had happened. The Goetic spirits he impersonated got quite angry about it…

The Conjurer

As mentioned above, the conjurer performs the majority of the work in an evocation. The Conjurer needs to have proficiency in working with circle creation rituals like the Lesser Banishing Rituals of the Pentagram (LBRP) and Hexagram (LBRH), the Greater Banishing Rituals of the Pentagram (GBRP) and Hexagram (GBRH), and the Opening by Watchtower. Your skill with these rituals defines the strength of your circle.

The Conjurer must also write up the appropriate orations necessary to perform the evocation. This includes a couple of conjurations, curses, and an oath. He should also write out questions and charges for the spirit beforehand to promote clarity of purpose and avoid confusion under pressure. On top of all this, the conjurer usually takes responsibility for acquiring all of the temple equipment necessary to perform the operation, such as the Triangle of evocation and the sigil of the spirit. Finally, the Conjurer needs to have good communication skills to work effectively with both the seer and the spirit.

The Seer

We cannot perceive the Etheric plane with our Material senses. Skrying involves attuning yourself to sense the Etheric plane and communicate with its inhabitants. Many Seers use a skrying medium, such as a crystal ball or a magick mirror, which serves as a portal through which the Seer can look into the Etheric Plane and communicate with the summoned spirit. Skrying primarily employs sight and hearing to gather information, but it may involve the other senses as well.

Some people have a natural talent for skrying, but most must work to develop the ability to see things beyond the Material realm. Anyone can develop the ability to skry using meditation and visualization practices. Many magical texts contain exercises that can help you develop into a competent Seer.[5]

The Seer enters a passive state of gnosis and looks through the skrying medium into the Etheric plane, communicating all information received to the Conjurer. This allows the Conjurer to focus on the more active elements of the operation, evocation and communication.

The Seer must strive to relay all information received to the Conjurer as clearly and directly as possible without filtering or reinterpreting it. Things that don't make any sense to the Seer often have special significance to the Conjurer. The spirit will speak to the Conjurer, and the Seer should relay dialogue in the first person whenever possible. (For example, saying "I have arrived," instead of "The spirit says it has arrived.") The Seer need only talk directly to the Conjurer to describe an image or emotion conveyed by the spirit.

Note that the Seer will often see and identify any problems that

---

5   I recommend the exercises included in Konstantinos' *Summoning Spirits*, pages 19-36.

may occur during the evocation before the Conjurer notices them. If the Seer feels uncomfortable in any way, she must relate this to the Conjurer. Let the Conjurer subdue and command the spirits. The Seer should never have to move from the passive role of skrying to the active role of a magician defending against malevolent spirits.

Other Roles

Sometimes more than two people will desire to perform a Goetic evocation. In fact, some sorcerers like to tackle the *Goetia* as a group project, with everyone taking turns as Conjurer and Seer. The group method allows everyone to quickly gain experience and practice.

Those who do not take on a role as one of the two operators may perform other functions within the temple. One person could act as an attendant to the Conjurer, taking responsibility for setting up the temple and assisting as needed. Another could serve as a scribe, operating an audio recorder and taking notes.

I suggest that those who do not play an active role in the evocation practice skrying and observe the evocation on the Etheric plane. The practice will help you hone your Etheric senses, and you can compare notes with the Seer after the evocation.

Visitors

Sometimes someone outside your standard group may desire to sit in on an evocation. For example, another magician may want to witness a Goetic evocation to gain a better understanding of the process, or a third party may have a vested interest in the purpose and outcome of a working. If you feel comfortable inviting visitors into your circle, make sure to lay down the law before the evocation so that your guests do not interfere with it in any way. The general rules include don't break the circle during the evocation, don't speak unless directly spoken to, and only address your concerns to the Conjurer, not the Seer and certainly not to the spirit unless prompted by the Conjurer.

THE GOETIC TEMPLE

To summon a spirit, grimoires often demand elaborate ceremonies performed with multiple tools prepared in the right way at the right time. Such unnecessary restrictions severely limit when and where we can perform our evocations. Keep it simple and evoke more often.

Most sorcerous evocations in Western Esotericism require only four tools: a magical circle, a Triangle, a skrying medium, and the sigil of the spirit you wish to work with.

The Magick Circle

The days of the physical magical circle have passed. These relics possess great power, but take great effort to make and require a large area to dedicate to them. Modern sorcerers prefer the convenience of creating an Etheric circle though the simple process of ritual. You will find circle creation rituals in many traditions that interact with spiritual entities, especially in Western Esotericism.

Circle creation rituals have three purposes. First, they operate as protective barriers and etheric boundaries, marking and clearing space in preparation for further work. Second, they generate energy that empowers the sorcerer and assists in the manifestation of the spirit. Third, they put the participants into an altered state of consciousness (gnosis) more conducive to interactions with spiritual entities.

The GBRP works well as a basic circle creation ritual. However, the more energy that you generate with the ritual, the stronger and clearer your spirit will manifest. Thus, the Mathers/ Crowley edition of the *Goetia* begins with the Bornless Ritual, which generates a great deal of energy and also establishes the sorcerer's dominion over the spirits. The Opening by Watchtower also generates a great deal of energy, drawing power from the Enochian rulers of the Elemental Watchtowers.

The Triangle

Many sorcerers simply regard the Triangle of evocation as a demonic spirit containment unit. However, it also serves as a podium for beneficent spirits as well. The sorcerer focuses the energy of the opening rituals into the Triangle, which provides the basis for the manifestation of the spirit.

This shape represents movement between dimensions, from a one-dimensional line to a two-dimensional shape, and from two-dimensional shape to a three-dimensional pyramid, the first regular solid. Divine and universal trinities form the core of many spiritual paths; we use the names of these trinities work to empower the Triangle.

These three names must have significance to the magician. When I performed my first evocation, calling up the Archangel Raphael, I asked him: "What do the names Primeumaton and

Anaphaxeton mean, and why do we put them on the Triangle?" I had used the traditional Solomonic Triangle to protect myself, yet I didn't even know what two of the three names meant!

To design your own Triangle, you must select three related names or words of power to inscribe on each side of the Triangle. The Solomonic Triangle uses Tetragrammaton, Anaphaxeton, and Primeumaton which represent God, the inverse of God, and that which balances out the two, analogous to thesis-antithesis-synthesis. I use the words of power from Lon DuQuette's Thelemic Triangle: Thelema, Agape, and Abrahadabra.[6] Whatever terms you use, they must resonate powerfully enough with you to constrain an unruly spirit.

The spirit will materialize in the circle at the center of the Triangle. For further protection from the spirit, the circle in the Solomonic Triangle has the name Archangel Michael inscribed upon it, the Archangel of Fire, Hod, and Evocation. I inscribed the name Ra-Hoor-Khuit, the fiery Lord of the New Aeon, around the circle in my first Triangle. You may not need a fourth name or word of power to help constrain the spirit, but it certainly doesn't hurt.

Construct the Triangle in any manner that you desire. You may paint the Triangle on wood or canvas; paper, metal, or even chalk will also work. In a bind, I once used duct tape to make a Triangle, and wrote the names and words of power on the tape with a black permanent ink pen. I designed my first Triangle on a computer, and then used a blueprint copier to enlarge the print to a useful size. You can mount a paper copy on foam board to give it more solidity if desired.

I recommend that you consecrate your Triangle before use. You will have to write your own ritual though, as the *Greater Key*

---

6   See Lon DuQuette's *Tarot of Ceremonial Magick* (York Beach, ME: Samuel Weiser, 1995), page 264.

of Solomon doesn't cover Triangles and the *Goetia* only gives us a description. Any ritual that activates the names on the Triangle and dedicates it to sorcerous operation will do. I have posted my own script on my website as an example.[7]

The Sigil

The Conjurer uses a sigil to establish an Etheric link with the spirit. Without that link, you might as well try to jump-start a dead horse with a car battery. A sigil serves as your principal means of identifying a spirit.

The Conjurer must prepare a sigil for use in the working. You may make this task as simple or as complex as you desire. Initially, keep the physical representation of the sigil simple. Once the spirit has a good track record, you can always construct a more elaborate sigil as a reward, using parchment and special inks for added effect. Heavy paper, mounting board, and small wooden disks all serve as practical media for sigils. For Elemental spirits, you may use flashing colors to enhance your sigil. Make your sigil large enough to use in evocation yet small enough to hide it away afterwards.

Many spirits (Goetic spirits in particular) want their sigils engraved in metal—it gives them a form of permanent presence on the Material plane and thus strengthens their objective identity. This also makes the sigils much more resistant to physical punishment unless you bring metalworking tools into your circle. I suggest that you hold off on such a task until you have established a relationship with the spirit and deemed it worthy of such an effort.

You activate or charge a sigil by using it in a successful evocation of the corresponding spirit. If desired, you may also

7   www.hermetic.com/osiris. "On the Triangle of Art."

activate the sigil before the evocation by consecrating it. I use a simple method based on elements of the Neophyte Ritual of the Golden Dawn. It requires a censer (or stick of incense) and a cup of water. Place the sigil upon your altar between the censer and cup and open your temple with the appropriate rituals.

Take the cup, make a cross over the sigil, and sprinkle the sigil with water while saying:

"I purify this sigil of the Spirit N with Water."

Please note that you do not need to drench the sigil; a single drop of water works to complete the purification.

Exchange the cup for the censer and make a cross over the sigil with the censer. Place the censer back on the altar, add some fresh incense to the coals, and hold the sigil in the smoke, saying:

"I consecrate this sigil of the Spirit N with Fire."

Then hold up the sigil with both hands and say:

"I do declare that I have duly purified and consecrated this sigil of the Spirit N, now ready for use in evocation."

Close the temple and put the sigil in a safe place until you perform the evocation.

The Skrying Medium

The skrying medium serves as your window into the Etheric plane. Popular skrying tools of old include the crystal ball (or shewstone, as Dee called it) and the magic mirror, essentially a piece of glass with a matte black background.

Many variations on this theme exist. One Seer I met hung a black sheet on the wall above the Triangle and used that surface as a skrying medium. Some authors suggest that the black circle at the center of the Solomonic Triangle actually represents a magic mirror used for skrying.[8]

I prefer to use a blindfold, which gives me an almost unlimited view, free from all visual distractions. Using a blindfold for skrying solves a number of common problems. It allows the Conjurer to use any light source he desires for the evocation without having to worry about reflections in the crystal or mirror distracting the Seer. A blindfolded Seer employs a medium only limited by her field of vision and that lacks most external distractions (i.e. the pictures on the wall, the Conjurer's bookshelf, etc.), making it easier to focus on the evocation. The Seer compensates for the fact that she cannot see the Triangle by visualizing it on the Etheric plane.

A blindfold also easily puts you in an altered state of consciousness, as I realized when hoodwinked at my Neophyte initiation into the Temple of Light and Darkness. The loss of vision disoriented me much more than I had anticipated, and I truly felt like a Wanderer in the Wild Darkness as I stumbled through the first part of the ritual. I later realized why—I had taken the blindfold from my personal evocation kit. When I put that blindfold on, I almost immediately go into skrying mode, where the ceiling and floor drop away into blackness. Good for skrying, not so good for walking around in circles.

If you seek to work with Elemental spirits, note that each of the four Elements works as a skrying medium. For Earth, use crystals or mirrors; for Air, incense smoke; for Water, look into a bowl of water or ink; and for Fire, gazing into any flame will work, from candle flame to bonfire. (Always use the utmost care when using fire in evocation, as it can easily get out of hand. You might want to have someone around with a fire extinguisher in case the tool shed catches fire while you sit in your backyard speaking with salamanders.)

---

8   You can find instructions for constructing this "Skrying Triangle" in Konstantinos' *Summoning Spirits* and Donald Michael Kraig's *Modern Magick* (St. Paul, MN: Llewellyn, 1988).

Other Useful Equipment

I have added another item to my personal list of required tools: a digital voice recorder. These wonderful devices allow us to keep complete and accurate records of our evocations. No more taking notes during the evocation or transcribing records from tape. Simply vocalize all sides of the conversation and any other details you want to record. You can download the recordings and store them on your computer, which makes magical record keeping much easier. Transcriptions or audio recordings come in very handy when evaluating Goetic evocations, for they let us review the exact wording of the spirit's charge.

You'll also need a blank book and a good pen with dark, easy-flowing ink to take notes and to record any non-verbal information the spirits may give you (i.e. sigils, diagrams, etc.) You should also have a copy of this book or your source grimoire with you in the circle in case you need to look something up.

The Conjurer may require additional temple equipment to properly conduct an opening ritual. For instance, to properly perform the Opening by Watchtower you need a set of Watchtower Tablets, a set of Elemental Weapons, and an altar.[9]

Use anything that creates a magical atmosphere to help empower your evocation. Many conjurers use robes (magical clothing), candles (magical lighting), and incense (magical scents) to create the proper setting for a magical working. You may also bring in anything else you desire for personal protection: Solomonic amulets, wands, symbols of power, binky, etc. I performed my first evocation brandishing a Wast scepter as a symbol of my will and authority.

Some magicians like to bring a sword with them when

---

9   Once you get the hang of it, you don't really need the altar and the Elemental Weapons. You can visualize the Weapons when you need them and dissolve them when you have finished. Note that each Weapon still requires a different grip; here lies the key to the effective use of this method.

Personally, I really dislike having an altar in the circle; it takes up too much space and just gets in the way of the Conjurer. I believe that the Conjurer belongs at the center of the circle, not an altar.

entering the Goetic temple, but you do not really need it. Easier ways to subdue spirits exist. I have found that flinging pentagrams (in the manner of Crowley's Star Ruby) at an unruly spirit works as effectively as poking it with your sword. Still, standing in a magick circle and conjuring a spirit with a sword in your hand truly gives you a sense of power and authority.

You can also use the sword to reach outside the magick circle without breaking it. You can stab, point, and even drag objects into the circle risk-free as long as you make sure that no part of your body leaves the protection of the circle.

RITUAL TIMING AND DIVINATION

Grimoires give detailed instructions for determining the all-important Right Time to consecrate tools and perform an evocation. Unfortunately, most formulae for determining ritual timing rely on the elaborate pseudoscience of astrology.

The roots of astrology lie in various ancient civilizations' misinterpretation of what they saw in the sky and the erroneous belief that the position of stars and planets somehow affects or reflects everything that happens here on Earth. However, this misunderstanding does not invalidate the existence of planetary energies. No one can deny that thousands of years of belief in astrology have created some very powerful spirits. I have worked with a few of them myself. But while I do believe that one can access the energy of Saturn and interact with Saturnian spirits, I do not believe that the movement or position of planet Saturn in the sky has any effect on what happens on Earth.

Astrological timing has too many limitations. Perform magick when you will or need to; don't wait for a Wednesday after the full Moon when Sun resides in Sagittarius. Besides, you already have the most versatile tool for planning evocations right within your grasp: the tarot.

Before performing an evocation of any spirit, do a short three-card divination to evaluate your charge and determine the general nature of the results. For example, "What would result if I performed an evocation of Orobas to help me find a new job?" The reading usually gives you enough information to determine (among other things) whether or not you've chosen a good time for your evocation. This method allows you to plan your evocations around your own schedule rather than that of the planets and stars. Think of all the time you will save, thanks to the tarot!

If you can't locate the service you desire in the Goetic Yellow Pages (Appendix Two), you may use thirty-six cards of the minor arcana (the numbered cards in the deck, minus the aces) to select a Goetic spirit. In the early twentieth century, magicians connected each card with one decan (10°) of the zodiacal wheel, and determined that two Goetic spirits rule each decan, one spirit for night and another for day. Remove the decan cards from the deck and shuffle them, making sure to invert some of the cards in the process. Ask the cards to give you the name of the spirit who may best accomplish your task, draw a card, and look up the spirit. Aright cards signify the day spirit, and reversed cards, the night spirit.

WANDS

Card	Day Spirit	Night Spirit
2	Bael	Phenex
3	Agares	Halphas
4	Vassago	Malphas
5	Beleth	Procel
6	Leraye	Furcas
7	Eligor	Balam
8	Glasya-Labolas	Zagan
9	Bune	Valak
10	Ronove	Andras

CUPS

Card	Day Spirit	Night Spirit
2	Buer	Bifrons
3	Gusoin	Vual
4	Sitri	Haagenti
5	Ipos	Amy
6	Aim	Orias
7	Naberius	Vapula
8	Furfur	Seer
9	Marchosias	Dantalion
10	Stolas	Andromalius

SWORDS

Card	Day Spirit	Night Spirit
2	Saleos	Orobas
3	Purson	Gemory
4	Morax	Ose
5	Foras	Amduscias
6	Asmoday	Belial
7	Gaap	Decarabia
8	Amon	Sabnack
9	Barbatos	Shax
10	Paimon	Vine

DISKS

Card	Day Spirit	Night Spirit
2	Berith	Flauros
3	Astaroth	Andrealphus
4	Forneus	Cimeies
5	Gamigim	Raum
6	Marbas	Focalor
7	Valefar	Vepar
8	Zepar	Alloces
9	Botis	Caim
10	Bathin	Murmur

After you have gained some experience working with Goetic spirits, ask the tarot this question: "Give me the name of the Goetic spirit who causes me the most harm." This generally leads to a difficult yet rewarding series of evocations.

Finally, if you just can't let go of astrology, the tarot possesses a great deal of astrological symbolism that you may interpret in any way you desire. For example, the Knight, Queen, and Prince cards of each suit represent three decans of the zodiac, and each Princess rules one quadrant (90° or three signs) of the zodiacal wheel. We have already mentioned the thirty-six decan cards. Please note that the planet-in-sign attributions given to the forty numbered cards of the tarot do not represent the full range of planet-sign combinations. The Golden Dawn created these attributions for symbolic value, not practical astrological use.

THE EVOCATION

The Evocation has five parts: the Opening, the Conjuration, the Reception, the Charge, and the Dismissal. You can find examples of traditional conjurations and other orations in most copies of the *Goetia*; the examples used here come from my own script.

Temple Setup

Put everything that you will need for the evocation near the center of the magick circle, where the Conjurer will stand during the operation. Place the Triangle anywhere just outside the boundary of the circle you will create; you may evoke Goetic spirits from any direction. The Seer sits on the floor or in a chair facing the Triangle.

I have found that in a standard temple space, where the walls correspond with the cardinal directions, it works best to place the Triangle in the least distracting corner of the room. This allows you to make the circle larger in most cases, and keeps the Seer out of the Conjurer's way during opening rituals that work with the cardinal directions.

The spirit's sigil belongs within the circle, where the Conjurer uses it to link with the spirit. Understand that the Seer should always avoid looking directly at an active sigil, lest she accidentally awaken that same spirit within her own consciousness.

Use natural lighting, either candles or an oil lamp. Make sure that the Conjurer has enough light to read by! After the operators have prepared themselves as they see fit (bathing, robing, one last trip to the bathroom, etc.), they should light any incense desired for the evocation and enter the circle.

The Opening

The evocation begins with a circle creation ritual, which, as noted above, serves to define boundaries, generate energy, and induce gnosis. You may perform the GBRP, or the Star Ruby and the Star Sapphire, or any other circle creation ritual that you have proficiency with. For those who prefer a more complicated and more powerful ritual, you may use the Opening by Watchtower to empower a Goetic evocation.[10]

The Bornless Ritual included by many Conjurers in Goetic evocations properly belongs to the Opening, as the ritual establishes a link between the Conjurer and his personal Daemon or Holy Guardian Angel (HGA). Liber Samekh, the Thelemic version of the Bornless Ritual, also works in this manner.

Many magicians establish a link with their personal Daemon before the Conjuration because it gives them additional power, protection, confidence, and authority. An invocation of one's personal Daemon does not require a ritual as complex as the Bornless Ritual; a simple acknowledgment and appeal will do, such as:

"I do invoke my personal Daemon to empower and protect me, that I may successfully perform this evocation."

Understand that the Conjurer does not need to have achieved Knowledge and Conversation of his personal Daemon to call upon it for help. No actual communication need take place at all. Make an honest and sincere effort to ask for your personal Daemon's help, the Daemon will do the rest.

---

10   See Appendix 3 in Part Five: The Watchtower System.

The Conjuration

Before reciting the conjuration, study the spirit's sigil until you feel an energetic link with the spirit. This technique resembles listening for a dial tone before making a telephone call. Stare at or through the sigil until it glows with energy. How do you know you have established the link? More often than not you get a "feeling" or a "knowing," although sometimes the spirit will respond verbally.

The basic conjuration answers five questions: what, who, where, how, and why:

What do you will to do? **I do evoke thee...**

Who do you will to evoke? **...O Spirit N!**

Where do you want the spirit to appear? **Manifest in the Triangle before me...**

How do you want the spirit to appear: **...in a pleasant and comely form...**

Why do you want to meet with the spirit? **...that I may converse with thee and employ thy services.**

To summarize:

I do evoke thee, O Spirit N! Manifest in the Triangle before me in a pleasant and comely form, that I may converse with thee and employ thy services.

Elaborate and embellish as desired.

Spirits usually appear the first time you summon them. If nothing manifests after a minute or so, repeat the conjuration. If the spirit still does not appear, you may compel it to appear by appealing to its superiors or to your own deities for help. I prefer to derive my power and authority from my own accomplishments as a magician and sorcerer:

"Hear me, O spirit N! I, Michael Osiris Snuffin, a mighty sorcerer and powerful magician, command you to appear before me! I have attained the Degree of Perfect Initiate in the Ordo Templi Orientis. I have seen the Vision of the Machinery of the Universe, and I stand at the Portal of the Adepts. I have spoken with the Archangel Raphael, and he hath brought me into balance. I have the blessings of Gabriel and Auriel, and the protection of Michael. By my own authority I do conjure thee and command you to manifest in the Triangle before me in a pleasant and comely form!"

Do not fluff up your magical resume here; the spirits will call you on it!

If the spirit still doesn't show up, you may have to resort to curses and threats of punishment to compel it to appear. Spirits compelled through the use of threats usually show up in a bad mood, so you may want to call the evocation off and try again in the future if you don't have the fight in you. Personally, I believe that if you have gone through this much trouble to set up the evocation, you might as well go through with it.

Do not use appearance to determine the identity of Goetic and other demonic spirits. The descriptions given in the *Goetia* and other grimoires mean little; these spirits usually appear as they will, sometimes in a form intended to intimidate or frighten. Simply ask them to assume a "pleasant and comely form" and they usually comply.

The Reception

Once the spirit manifests in the Triangle, verify its identity. The best methods of checking ID involve the use of names. Ask the spirit to identify itself; do not reveal the name of the desired spirit until it has had a chance to speak. Ask the spirit to sign its name in the skrying medium; specify English or otherwise the name may appear in an unfamiliar language. Vibrating the spirit's name or the name of its superior will energize the spirit and may improve the quality of its manifestation.

If you still have doubts, ask the spirit to swear an oath of identity:

"Do you swear to answer to this name and sigil, and agree to perform the functions assigned to it?"

If the spirit firmly and unambiguously agrees to this, then you may continue, regardless of whether the spirit originally gave the right name or not.

Once you have verified its identity, politely welcome the spirit. Note that you need not thank the spirit for coming, as it probably didn't do so of its own accord.

After verification, you must compel the spirit to swear an Oath on its name and sigil. You need to command the spirit to swear to speak truthfully with you, to carry out your orders without delay, and to avoid harming you or anyone else in the process. For example:

"I command you to swear on your name and sigil to answer my questions truthfully, without omitting or editing any information in communication, and to perform any tasks that I command you to perform without delay or hesitation. Furthermore, you will swear to accomplish these tasks in a manner that does not tempt me to violate

my own morals or my True Will, in a manner that harms no one, neither man nor woman nor beast unless I specifically command you to do so. Do you swear to abide by this Oath?"

Do not allow spirits to negotiate the terms of the Oath! I have called up a few spirits who refused at first or had a few questions, but they all swore to the Oath in the end. If the Conjurer cannot get the spirit nailed down on this one, then you must resort to curses and punishments (see below) or abort the operation and banish.

Why do I include an exception clause in the second part of the Oath? Because sometimes spirits must harm living things in order to carry out their charge. To cure many types of illness, viruses, bacteria and cancerous cells must perish. To rid your house of pests usually involves killing insects or small mammals. To get that promotion at work, another person will have to stay put. You get the idea.

The Charge

You have completed the evocation and you have the spirit's attention; now the real work begins. You have established the terms of your relationship with the spirit, and now you must give it something to do.

This brings up an important point: do not call up a Goetic spirit without a task in mind. Suppose that someone compelled you to drive across the country to meet them, and when you arrived at their doorstep, they said "Welcome! I just wanted to see if you actually existed and if you would really show up. Bye!" How would you feel when they closed the door in your face? I'd feel pissed! If you call up a spirit and don't give it something to do, it will often find something to do. This may explain why some Conjurers have trouble with Goetic spirits.

If you want the spirit to do something for you, you must issue a charge to the spirit. A good charge resembles a business contract. It describes the services provided by the spirit and the desired outcome, and includes a deadline for completion and terms of payment. You will use this information later to determine the success or failure of your evocation, so make sure to keep a record of it.

CONSIDER THESE GENERAL GUIDELINES FOR WORKING WITH GOETIC SPIRITS:

• **Speak politely and respectfully to the spirits** and they will usually respond in kind. Aleister Crowley sums up the point in Liber Librae:

> "Therefore fear not the Spirits, but be firm and courteous with them; for thou hast no right to despise or revile them; and this too may lead thee astray. Command and banish them, curse them by the Great Names if need be; but neither mock nor revile them, for so assuredly wilt thou be led into error."[11]

Goetic and other demonic spirits often require an attitude of command and authority if you expect to get anywhere. Childish, obnoxious, or immature behavior just makes the evocation more difficult. This doesn't mean that you can't threaten an unruly spirit, just that you must use a little tact and maturity when doing so.

• **Keep your charges realistic;** don't ask for the impossible. Goetic spirits can do some incredible things, but just like any other form of magic, Goetic spirits must work within the laws

---

11   Aleister Crowley, *Liber ABA: Book Four, Parts I-IV* (York Beach, ME: Samuel Weiser, 2000), page 668.

of the Material universe. For instance, I understand that actual physical invisibility takes years of work and practice to pull off.[12] If you have questions as to whether or not a spirit can perform the task that you desire, ask.

Don't make the spirit's charge unnecessarily difficult to carry out. If you command a spirit to get you laid and then hide in your apartment for the next two weeks, things probably won't work out.

• **Give specific and unambiguous orders.** If you want money, let the spirit know how much. If you want the answer to a specific question, write it out before the Evocation. If you desire sex, let the spirit know what standards you have.

Keep in mind that using too much detail can work against you. Asking a spirit to procure you a working car requires much less effort than asking it to find you a 1957 lime green Dodge Dart in mint condition by tomorrow. Again, if you make things too hard or impossible for the spirit, you will only see failure after failure.

• **Set firm deadlines** so you can gauge whether the spirit has accomplished its charge. If you give a spirit a long-term or continuous charge, set up an appointment to touch bases in the future to discuss progress.

• **If you receive legal, medical, or financial advice, consider the source** and preferably get a second (human) opinion before taking significant action. Spirits can make mistakes just like the rest of us. In a world where nothing has absolute truth and anything can happen, even deities can fail to deliver.

• **Don't let Goetic spirits intimidate you.** Some spirits will try to talk you into or out of something you may not need, or into doing something you will regret later. If they ask something

---

12   A note on invisibility: this ability works on the Material plane to create a mental and social invisibility, where people just don't see you and tend to ignore you unless they specifically seek you out. I understand that you may also achieve Etheric invisibility, which masks your Etheric body and makes you very difficult to find.

of you that makes you uncomfortable, then don't do it! If you don't want to make an on-the-spot decision, dismiss the spirit and consider the request, then call up the spirit when you feel ready to give it an answer.

• **Every Goetic spirit has its niche,** something that it can do very well that has great value to you. The challenge of Goetic sorcery lies in finding each spirit's niche. Likewise, most Goetic spirits feel happier when employed for productive and important services. In many ways, working with the *Goetia* resembles a large spiritual rehabilitation project.

• **Remember that true magicians always take responsibility for their actions**, and that includes the actions of the spirits under their control. Asking or commanding spirits to do your dirty work does not absolve you of responsibility! As one spirit put it, "The blood comes back to you." To use a more extreme example: we have no records that prove Adolf Hitler personally killed anyone, and yet his ability to incite others to commit acts of terror, murder, and genocide has made him a modern icon of evil. In the end, he killed himself rather than face the consequences of his actions. Take responsibility or it will overtake you.

• **When it comes to working with demonic spirits, quality always trumps quantity.** Those claiming to have evoked every spirit of the *Goetia* probably actually know only a handful of them, for building stable relationships with any entity (Material or Etheric) takes time and effort. While the shotgun method of sorcery will often produce results, it usually creates too much collateral damage in the process; evoking large numbers of demonic spirits without getting to know them first increases the possibility for problems and makes it much harder to track down unruly spirits.

I originally believed in Aleister Crowley's theory that Goetic spirits represented unused parts of the human brain. Then I met a few people who claimed to have called up and bound all seventy-two spirits of the *Goetia*, and as they demonstrated no special talents, extraordinary powers, or massive wealth, I now have serious doubts about the spirit-brain connection.

The Dismissal

When you feel satisfied that the spirit understands the terms and conditions of the charge, dismiss the spirit:

"I dismiss you, O spirit N. Go back unto your errands and habitations in peace. This evocation has ended."

Again, embellish as desired.

When the Seer confirms that the spirit has departed, close the evocation with a banishing circle creation ritual. Make sure that the spirit has departed before you break the circle.

You have now activated the spirit's sigil by using it in a successful evocation; it has an Etheric link to the spirit. Therefore, you need to keep the sigil in a safe place where no one will disturb it. The Oath protects you from the malice of the spirit, but anyone else who sees the sigil might accidentally activate the spirit to their own detriment. Many Conjurers have a special box or pouch that they store their activated sigils in to keep them safe. Put your sigil away and let the spirit do its work.

If the desired results fail to manifest within the given time, you may call up the spirit and ask for an explanation. But before you pull out your Triangle, you might want to review the spirit's charge. Sometimes you will find that the spirit did exactly what you told it to do, as opposed to what you wanted it to do. Things will not always work out the way you expected. Keep that in mind before you start punishing spirits and burning sigils.

If the spirit succeeds in fulfilling its charge, call it up, thank it, and give it something else to do. Do not forget to honor promised rewards for services; spirits always remember, and some may remind you in unpleasant or disruptive ways. If you do not wish to continue working with the spirit, end the relationship in a formal manner. Sorcerers consider it unwise to leave such loose ends hanging in the Etheric world.

PAYMENT FOR SERVICES

Some sorcerers don't compensate Goetic spirits for their service, commanding them to serve as slaves. I prefer to treat the spirits like employees, offering energy in exchange for service, a more equitable arrangement. Besides, most Goetic spirits don't want to work for free, and they generally perform better when treated well and offered incentives. Every once in a while you'll call up a spirit that accepts the old "as I evolve, so shall ye evolve" rationalization, but most won't buy it. Goetic spirits perform services in exchange for energy.

You can pay spirits directly by raising energy on the Etheric plane and channeling it to the spirit through its sigil. You can also perform actions on the Material plane that strengthen the spirit's objective identity. Goetic spirits appear to suffer from an objective identity crisis, and thus prefer promises of material payment.

Simple rewards employ the spirit's name. Where your attention goes, your energy flows. Praise the spirit in the company of other sorcerers, or mention your relationship in public. Write a poem or song that uses the spirit's name, or incorporate a spirit's sigil into artwork.

Another type of reward involves improving the spirit's sigil. You may create a more artistic version of the sigil using special paints or inks to show your appreciation. Save the ultimate sigil improvement project, etching the sigil on a metal disk, for spirits that have a proven track record.

I reward helpful spirits by painting their sigil on the glass of seven-day candle of a requested color, then burning the candle until exhausted. The flame generates energy for the spirit; more importantly, I don't leave unattended candles burning (and neither should you), so my sigil-candles receive a great deal of attention as I extinguish and relight them many times. The sigil-candles also get real estate on my Goetic altar, a place of honor.

Don't hesitate to get creative! One spirit that helped me find a much-needed job received a small dinner party in its honor, which included a place setting at the table for the spirit. Another sorcerer I know painted a very striking picture of a faithful spirit that she uses in evocation and places on her altar in recognition of its fine work.

Do make sure that the reward reflects the difficulty and quality of the service rendered. When I first started working with the *Goetia*, I grossly overpaid spirits for small tasks until the Archangel Michael set me straight. A spirit that brings in a little extra cash deserves different treatment than a spirit that lands you your dream job. Reward responsibly!

CURSES AND PUNISHMENTS

One question remains: What do you do with a stubborn and uncooperative spirit, or what if it fails to carry out its charge?

First, you start in with the curses (threats). Tell the spirit that if it does not do as you command, you will punish it, using either divine authority or your own. If you threaten a spirit with punishment, make sure that you feel willing and able to go through with it. Idle threats will not work here. If the spirit still refuses to comply, then you must punish it for its disobedience.

To punish a Goetic spirit, the *Goetia* instructs us to "write thou his seal on parchment and put thou it into a strong black box; with brimstone, assafoetida, and such like things that bear a stinking smell; and then bind the box up round with an iron wire, and hang it upon the point of thy sword, and hold it over the fire of charcoal" while reciting "The Conjuration of the Fire."[13]

These instructions may seem impracticable and unnecessarily complex, but they illustrate an important point: what you do to the activated sigil has a direct effect on the spirit. Putting the sigil in a foul smelling box irritates the spirit. Singeing the sigil singes the spirit. Piercing the sigil with a pin or lancet will cause pain to the spirit. You get the idea.

Let me give you a personal example. One of the first spirits I conjured gave me a lot of trouble, twisting my words around for sake of argument and only reluctantly agreeing to the Oath after much debate. He failed to carry out the task I charged him with, and when I called him up to talk to him about it, he made it very clear that he did not want to work with me at that time.[14] So I drew his sigil on a small piece of paper, put it in a vial of water, and stuck it in the freezer. In essence, I froze the spirit, binding

---

13 Crowley, Aleister, ed. *The Goetia: The Lesser Key of Solomon the King*, page 86. This method never made sense to me, as the stinking smell also punishes the Conjurer and Seer.

14 He summarized his attitude toward me in one sentence: "I understand that you are but an apprentice... I will wait until your wings dry."

him until I felt ready and willing to deal with him again.

The ultimate punishment for an uncooperative spirit involves ceremonially burning the activated sigil and never calling upon the spirit again, never even acknowledging its existence. As noted above, Goetic spirits love attention, and by destroying the sigil you affirm that you will never pay attention to the spirit again. **Ever.**

This brings us to a most effective threat. If a Goetic spirit refuses to cooperate, tell it that you will dismiss it and call up another spirit that can actually get the job done. Spirits often have a sudden change of heart when threatened with sincere rejection.

CONCLUSION

Now that you know how to perform an evocation, the time has come to move from theory to practice. To aid you in this task, I have included some resources for preparing and performing your own Goetic evocations.

Appendix 1 gives an outline of the main elements that comprise a Goetic evocation as presented in this manual. You may use it as a checklist for your first few evocations.

Appendix 2 contains the Goetic Yellow Pages, a directory of services offered in the *Goetia* and the identification numbers of the spirits that can perform them. Of course, if you have any questions about whether or not a spirit can perform a specific task, just ask it.

Appendix 3 presents a transcription of an actual Goetic evocation I performed as a member of a conjuring group. Many of the evocations I have performed have not gone as smoothly as this one, but it does serve as a good example of a standard evocation.

APPENDIX I:
OUTLINE OF A GOETIC EVOCATION

0. Preparation

    a. The Triangle

    b. The skrying medium.

    c. The sigil of the desired spirit.

    d. Other equipment: Goetia, blank book, pen, digital recorder, protective devices (sword, amulets, etc.), temple equipment for opening rituals.

1. The Opening

    a. Create a ritual circle.

    b. Invoke personal Daemon or HGA.

2. The Conjuration

    a. Study sigil of spirit until you establish a link.

    b. Recite conjuration. If spirit does not appear, recite second conjuration or curses.

3. The Reception

    a. Ask the spirit to identify itself.

    b. Command it to swear to answer to the name and sigil and to perform the duties ascribed to it.

    c. Command it to swear to an oath to speak truthfully, to carry out your orders without delay, and to not harm you or anyone else.

4. The Charge

    a. Converse with the spirit and command it to carry out a particular service.

5. The Dismissal

    a. Dismiss spirit.

    b. Close with appropriate banishing rituals.

APPENDIX 2
THE GOETIC YELLOW PAGES

Services	Spirit Numbers
Answers truthfully of secret things	5, 9, 11, 20, 23, 26, 29, 32, 34, 35, 55, 57, 64, 70, 71
Arithmetic	32
Arson	23
Astrology	46, 50, 58, 59
Astronomy	21, 32, 36, 52, 65
Bend trees	67
Boldness	22
Build towers/castles/cities	38, 39, 43, 45
Cause hatred/arguments/ discord	33, 53, 63
Cause disease	5
Cause storms/change weather	34, 41, 42, 45
Cure disease	5, 10
Change places of the dead	26, 46
Chiromancy	50
Declare past/present/future	3, 7, 8, 11, 15, 17, 20, 22, 25, 28, 29, 33, 40, 45, 47, 51, 53, 55, 56, 64
Destroy cities	23, 40, 45
Destroy dignities	2, 40
Destroy enemies/murder	25, 39, 41, 42, 43, 64, 72
Dignities/prelacies	9, 11, 24, 28, 30, 55, 59, 68
Earthquakes	2
Eloquence	26, 31

Ethics	31
Familiars	6, 9, 10, 20, 21, 27, 33, 39, 43, 44, 52, 58, 67, 68
Find lost/hidden things	3, 15, 20, 31, 44, 45, 66
Find person/thief	2, 70, 72
Friendships/reconcile friends and foes	7, 8, 11, 17, 25, 27, 30, 40, 47, 55 59, 68
Geometry	32, 46, 49, 65
Grammar	66
Handicrafts/professions	32, 60
Hidden treasure/wealth	8, 20, 26, 31, 32, 40, 44, 56, 58, 62, 66, 70, 72
Illusions, sound/vision	42, 49, 66, 69, 71
Infertility	16
Invisibility	1, 25, 31, 32, 51
Languages/tongues	2, 27, 30
Liberal arts and sciences	4, 9, 10, 21, 24, 25, 29, 32, 33, 37, 46, 49, 52, 57, 58, 60, 71
Logic	10, 31, 50, 66
Long life	31
Love of men and women	7, 12, 13, 16, 19, 33, 34, 47, 56, 71
Make people insensible	33, 44
Mechanical arts	5
Mind control	9, 71
Necromancy	4, 26, 46, 54
Philosophy	10, 33, 50, 54, 60
Poetry	37
Possession	20

Putrefy wounds	14, 42, 43
Pyromancy	50
Return stolen goods	72
Rhetoric	24, 27, 30, 50, 66
Serpents	62
Speak with animals/birds	8, 53
Transform people/shape shifting	5, 57, 59, 65, 66
Transmute water/wine/blood	48, 61
Transport men/things quickly	18, 33, 44, 70
Turn metals into gold	28, 48
Turn metals into coin (money)	61
Virtues of herbs/plants/ precious stones	10, 18, 21, 31, 36, 46, 49, 69
War/soldiers/bloodshed	14, 15, 25, 35, 38, 41, 42
Warm waters/discover baths	49
Wisdom	26, 48, 61
Wittiness	22, 23, 31, 51, 61

APPENDIX 3
AN EVOCATION OF GLASYA-LABOLAS

2/12/01, 10:05-10:20 p.m.
[S. was the Seer. LBRP, LBRH. I concentrated on consecrated sigil until a link was established.]

> *I conjure thee, O Glasya-Labolas! Manifest in the Triangle before me in a pleasant and comely form that I may converse with thee and employ thy services!*
>
> *[I just see fire.]*
>
> *O spirit, I do command thee to assume a more pleasant and comely (preferably human) form, that we may converse with thee and employ thy services!*
>
> *[OK.]*
>
> *What does he look like?*
>
> *[It has a round head and a hunchback-looking body.]*
>
> *Identify yourself.*
>
> *I am Glasya-Labolas.*
>
> *Glasya-Labolas, do you swear to answer to this name and to this sigil and agree to perform the functions ascribed thereof?*
>
> *I will answer to the name and the sigil.*
>
> *Then I do welcome thee, O Glasya-Labolas. But before we can work any further, I do require you to swear an oath.*
> *I command you to swear on your name and sigil to answer my questions truthfully, without omitting or editing any information in communication, and to perform any tasks that I command you to perform without delay or hesitation. Furthermore, you will swear to*

accomplish these tasks in a manner that does not tempt me to violate my own morals or my own True Will, in a manner that harms no one, neither man nor woman nor beast unless I specifically command you to do so. Do you swear to abide by this Oath?

    I, Glasya-Labolas, swear to this oath and will abide by you.

Then we can do business.

    We can.

Glasya-Labolas, it says here in the Goetia that you can cause love of both friends and of foes. Is this not true?

    [He's laughing but he's answering yes.]

We, the conjuring group, we call upon you to help us to find more people to be in our conjuring group. Can you do such a task?

    I can, but what would you do with more people?

We're not looking for just any "more people." We're looking for people who are serious about practicing and learning and exploring the art of evocation, and we are having trouble finding people like that.

    Just evocation?

Speaking for myself, magick in general; but in this case evocation in particular. We would like to have more people with which to work with, more people to contribute to this group, more people that can teach and that can learn. And we have called upon you to attract more people to this group, that we may be successful... and prosper.

    I can find more students but I don't know if I can find teachers. They're hard to come by and it's a rare thing.

Serious students are welcome. We can find many dabblers, people who wish to witness such a ceremony but have no true interest in performing *it or really learning anything from it themselves.*

I can help turn dabblers into serious students.

Do so if you wish, but do not go against anybody's will, as stated in the oath. All that we wish is for more serious people to join this group, to contribute to it, and we ask that you attract people to do so.

You only want four people?

No, I would like more people.

I want recognition.

Excuse me?

I want recognition.

Well, then you have a golden opportunity, because you are the first Goetic spirit this group has called up. If you perform well for us, we'll continue to use you, continue to praise your name. If you are agreeable, we will even give you offerings. But you must prove yourself first.

After I bring students, I would like you to say my name.

That's not a problem. If you bring more students into this group, more people to this group, they may be saying your name.

Leave my name in the library.

Your name in the library? How do you suggest we do so?

Written.

Where shall we put it?

In books.

Write it in books?

No. On parchment, and leave it in books for other people to find.

And what will happen when they find these names?

> *It can help bring more students, but it would also encourage more people to find me and I'd get more recognition that way.*

This I can do. I will write your name on a few pieces of parchment and put them in selected books within our library.

> *Excellent.*

Now the only thing left is to work on time and scheduling.

> *I'll need a lot of time to find more people in this area.*

How much time?

> *Six months. Maybe longer.*

I will give you six months, but I may check back with you in three.

> *You can check back with me in a month.*

Then why don't we do that. As an exercise for this group, we'll check back with you in a month. We'll talk a little bit about your progress, and anything further that needs to be done. We may even have another task for you.

> *When you bring dabblers into your circle, call my name afterwards and if they are serious, they'll come back.*

OK. Is there anything else?

> *No, but don't forget the parchment.*

It shouldn't be a problem. I believe I have some papyrus at home. Any particular color?

> *No.*

OK. Then it is settled.

> *It is settled.*

You will help us find some serious students, serious practitioners...

I will find students.

You will find some students. Just as long as they're serious students—that's what matters.

Agreed.

There is nothing more that needs to be said. I thank you, O Glasya-Labolas, for coming here before us and speaking with us. I do dismiss you. Go back unto your errands and your habitations, and shall I call upon you again be thou quick to respond. Now go!

[*He's gone.*]

[LBRP, LBRH. Closed the temple.]

CHAPTER FOUR

Spirits of the Goetia

The information listed here includes only the physical descriptions of the Goetic spirits and the services they perform. I have edited out extraneous information not pertinent to practical work, such as worthless feudal titles, inconsistent astrological data, and misleading character judgments by superstitious exorcists. You may find the full descriptions of the Goetic spirits in many books as well as online if so desired.

1. **BAEL.** He appears in diverse shapes, sometimes like a cat, sometimes like a toad, and sometimes human, and sometimes in all these forms at once. He speaks hoarsely. He can make people go invisible. He governs 66 legions of spirits.

2. **AGARES.** He appears in the form of a fair old human riding upon a crocodile, very mildly carrying a goshawk upon his fist. He makes them run that stand still, and fetches back runaways. He can teach all languages or tongues. He has power to destroy dignities, both supernatural and temporal, and causes earthquakes. He governs 31 legions of spirits.

3. VASSAGO. He appears in the same form as AGARES. He declares things past and to come, and discovers all hidden or lost things. He governs 26 legions of spirits.

4. GAMIGIM. He appears in the form of a little horse or ass, but changes into human shape at the request of the sorcerer. He speaks with a hoarse voice. He teaches all liberal sciences, and gives account of dead souls that died in sin. He governs 30 legions of spirits.

5. MARBAS. He appears at first in the form of a great lion, but puts on human shape at the request of the sorcerer. He answers truly of hidden or secret things. He causes diseases and cures them. He gives great wisdom and knowledge in mechanical arts, and changes people into other shapes. He governs 36 legions of spirits.

6. VALEFAR. He appears in the form of a lion with a human head, howling. He makes a good familiar, but tempts those he serves to steal. He governs 10 legions of spirits.

7. AMON. He first appears like a wolf with a serpent's tail, vomiting out of his mouth flames of fire; but at the command of the sorcerer, he puts on a human shape with a raven's head beset with dog's teeth. He tells all things past and to come. He procures love, and reconciles controversies between friends and foes. He governs 40 legions of spirits.

8. BARBATOS. He appears with four noble kings and their companions in great troops. He gives the understanding of the singing of birds, and the voices of other creatures, such as the barking of dogs. He breaks open hidden treasures laid by the enchantments of magicians. He knows all things past and to come, and reconciles friends and those in power. He governs 30 legions of spirits.

9. PAIMON. He appears in human form, sitting upon a dromedary, with a crown most glorious upon his head. He has a great voice, and roars at his first coming. There goes before him a host of spirits, like men with trumpets, well-sounding cymbals, and all other sorts of musical instruments. This spirit can teach all arts and sciences, and other secret things. He can reveal unto you the nature of the earth, and what holds it up in the waters; and the nature of the wind, or where it blows; or any other thing you may desire to know. He gives dignities and confirms the same. He binds or makes people subject unto the sorcerer. He gives good familiars, and as such can teach all arts. He governs 200 legions of spirits.

10. BUER. He appears in the shape of a centaur. He teaches moral and natural philosophy, the logical arts, and the virtues of all herbs and plants. He heals all distempers, and gives good familiars. He governs 50 legions of spirits.

11. GUSOIN. He appears like a xenophilus. He tells all things past, present, and to come, and shows the meaning of all questions you may ask. He reconciles friends, and gives honors and dignities. He governs 40 legions of spirits.

12. SITRI. He appears at first with a leopard's face and wings as a griffin; but at the command of the sorcerer he puts on a very beautiful human shape. He enflames people with love, and causes them to show themselves naked. He governs 60 legions of spirits.

13. BELETH or BILETH. He rides on a pale horse, with trumpets and all other kinds of musical instruments playing before him. Beleth causes love of both men and women, until the sorcerer has had his desires fulfilled. He governs 85 legions of spirits.

14. LERAYE or LERAJE. He appears as an archer clad in green, carrying a bow and quiver. He causes all great battles and contests, and causes arrow wounds to putrefy. He governs 30 legions of spirits.

15. ELIGOR. He appears in the form of a goodly knight carrying a lance, an ensign, and a serpent. He discovers hidden things, and knows things to come, and of wars, and how the soldiers will meet. He causes the love of lords and great persons. He governs 60 legions of spirits.

16. ZEPAR. He appears in red apparel and armed like a soldier. He causes women to love men, and brings them together in love. He also makes them barren. He governs 26 legions of spirits.

17. BOTIS. He appears at first in the form of an ugly viper, but at the command of the sorcerer he puts on a human shape with great teeth and two horns, carrying a sharp bright sword in his hand. He tells all things past and to come, and reconciles friends and foes. He governs 60 legions of spirits.

18. BATHIN. He appears like a strong human with the tail of a serpent, sitting upon a pale-colored horse. He knows the virtues of herbs and precious stones, and can transport people suddenly from one country to another. He governs 30 legions of spirits.

19. SALEOS or SALLOS. He appears in the form of a gallant, peaceful soldier wearing a duke's crown and riding on a crocodile. He causes love between women and men. He governs 30 legions of spirits.

20. PURSON. His appears commonly like a human with a lion's face, carrying a cruel viper in his hand, and riding upon a bear. Trumpets herald his arrival. He knows hidden things, can discover treasure, and tells all things past, present, and to come. He can take a body either human or aerial, and answers truly of all earthly things both secret and divine, and of the creation of the world. He brings forth good familiars. He governs 22 legions of spirits.

 **21. MORAX or MARAX.** He appears like a great bull with a human face. He makes people very knowing in astronomy and all the other liberal sciences; he gives good and wise familiars that know the virtues of herbs and precious stones. He governs 30 legions of spirits.

 22. IPOS. He appears in the form of an angel with a lion's head, goose's feet, and a hare's tail. He knows things past and to come. He makes people witty and bold. He governs 36 legions of spirits.

 23. AIM. He appears in the form of a very handsome human, but with three heads: the first like a serpent, the second human-like with two stars on his forehead, and the third like a cat. He rides on a viper, carrying a firebrand in his hand, with which he sets cities, castles, and great places on fire. He makes people witty in all manner of ways, and gives true answers unto private matters. He governs 26 legions of spirits.

 **24. NABERIUS.** He appears in the form of a black crow, fluttering about the circle, and speaks with a hoarse voice. He makes people cunning in all arts and sciences, but especially in the art of rhetoric. He restores lost dignities and honors. He governs 19 legions of spirits.

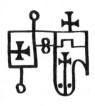

25. GLASYA-LABOLAS. He shows himself in the form of a dog with wings like a griffin. He teaches all arts and sciences in an instant, and causes bloodshed and manslaughter. He tells all things past and to come. He causes the love of friends and of foes. He can make a person go invisible. He governs 36 legions of spirits.

26. BUNE or BIME. He appears in the form of a dragon with three heads: one like a dog, one like a griffin, and one human. He speaks with a high and comely voice. He changes the places of the dead, and causes the spirits under him to gather together upon their sepulchers. He gives riches to a person, and makes him wise and eloquent. He gives true answers to your demands. He governs 30 legions of spirits.

27. RONOVE. He appears in the form of a monster. He teaches the art of rhetoric, and he gives good servants, knowledge of tongues, and favors of friends or foes. He governs 19 legions of spirits.

28. BERITH, BEAL, or BOLFRY. He appears like a soldier with red clothing riding upon a red horse and wearing a crown of gold. He speaks with a very clear and subtle voice. He gives true answers of things past, present, and to come. He can turn all metals into gold. He can give dignities and confirms them to people. He governs 26 legions of spirits.

29. **ASTAROTH.** He appears in the form of an unbeautiful angel riding on an infernal-like dragon, and carrying in his right hand a viper. He gives true answers of things past, present, and to come, and discovers all secrets. He makes people knowing in all liberal sciences. He governs 40 legions of spirits.

30. **FORNEUS.** He appears in the form of a great sea monster. He teaches the art of rhetoric. He can cause you to have a good name, and to have the knowledge of tongues. He makes people beloved of their foes as well as they love their friends. He governs 29 legions of spirits.

31. **FORAS.** He appears in the form of a strong human. He can give understanding to people how they may know the virtues of all herbs and precious stones. He teaches the arts of logic and ethics in all their parts. He makes people invisible, witty, eloquent and to live long. He can discover treasures and recover lost things. He governs 29 legions of spirits.

32. **ASMODAY or ASMODAI.** He appears with three heads, the first like a bull, the second human, and the third like a ram; with a serpent's tail, belching or vomiting up flames of fire out of his mouth. He has webbed feet like those of a goose. He sits upon an infernal dragon, carrying a lance and flag in his hands. He gives the ring of virtues; he teaches the arts of arithmetic, geometry, astronomy, and all other handicrafts. He gives full and true answers to your demands. He makes people invisible. He shows the place where treasures lie, and guards it. He governs 72 legions of spirits.

33. GAAP. He appears in a human shape, going before four great and mighty kings as if conducting them along in their way. He makes people knowing in philosophy and all the liberal sciences. He can cause love or hatred and make people insensible. He delivers familiars out of the custody of other magicians, and answers truly and perfectly of things past, present, and to come. He can carry and recarry people most speedily from one kingdom to another. He governs 66 legions of spirits.

34. FURFUR. He appears in the form of a hart with a fiery tail; but he will take on the form of an angel at the command of the sorcerer. He speaks with a hoarse voice. He will wittingly make love between man and woman. He can raise thunders, lightnings, blasts, and great tempestuous storms. He gives true answers of both secret and divine things if commanded. He governs 26 legions of spirits.

35. MARCHOSIAS. He appears at first in the form of a wolf, having griffin's wings and a serpent's tail, and vomiting up fire out of his mouth; but he puts on human shape at the command of the sorcerer. He has a strong fighting spirit. He gives true answers to all questions. He governs 30 legions of spirits.

 **36. STOLAS.** He first appears in the shape of a mighty raven, but changes into human shape at the command of the sorcerer. He teaches the art of astronomy and the virtues of herbs and precious stones. He governs 26 legions of spirits.

 **37. PHENEX or PHOENIX.** He appears like the bird phoenix, having a child's voice, but puts on human shape at the command of the sorcerer. He will speak marvelously of all wonderful sciences. He teaches poetry. He governs 20 legions of spirits.

 38. HALPHAS or MALTHAS. He appears in the form of a stock-dove, and he speaks with a hoarse voice. He builds up towers, and furnishes them with ammunition and weapons, and sends men-of-war to appointed places. He governs 26 legions of spirits.

 **39. MALPHAS.** He appears at first like a crow, but will put on human shape at the command of the sorcerer. He speaks with a hoarse voice. He can build houses and high towers, and can bring artificers together from all places of the world. He can destroy your enemies' desires or thoughts, and all that they have done. He gives good familiars. He governs 40 legions of spirits.

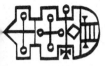

40. RAUM. He appears at first in the form of a crow; but puts on human shape at the command of the sorcerer. His will steal treasures out of king's houses and carry it where commanded; destroy cities and dignities; tell all things past, present, and to come; and cause love between friends and foes. He governs 30 legions of spirits.

41. FOCALOR or FORCALOR. He appears in a human form with griffin's wings. He kills people, drowns them in the waters, and overthrows ships of war, for he has power over both winds and seas; but he will not hurt any person or thing if commanded to the contrary by the sorcerer. He governs 30 legions of spirits.

42. VEPAR. She appears like a mermaid. She guides the waters, and guides ships laden with armor thereon. She can make the seas rough and stormy and to appear full of ships. Also she causes people to die in three days by putrefying their sores and wounds, and causing worms to breed in them. She governs 29 legions of spirits.

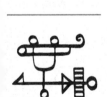

43. SABNACK. He appears in the form of an armed soldier with a lion's head, riding on a pale-colored horse. He builds high towers, castles and cities, and furnishes them with armor; and afflicts people for several days with wounds and with sores rotten and full of worms. He gives good familiars. He governs 50 legions of spirits.

44. SHAX. He appears in the form of a stock-dove, speaking with a hoarse and subtle voice. He takes away the sight, hearing, or understanding of any man or woman; and steals money out of king's houses. He will fetch horses or any other thing at the request of the sorcerer. He discovers all things hidden and not kept by wicked spirits. He gives good familiars, sometimes. He governs 30 legions of spirits.

45. VINE. He appears in the form of a lion riding upon a black horse, with a viper in his hand. He discovers hidden things, witches, and things present, past, and to come. He can build towers, throw down great stone walls, and make waters rough with storms. He governs 35 legions of spirits.

46. BIFRONS. He appears in the form of a monster, but puts on human shape at the command of the sorcerer. He makes one knowing in astrology, geometry, and other arts and sciences. He teaches the virtues of precious stones and woods. He changes dead bodies and puts them in another's place, and lights candles upon the graves of the dead. He governs 60 legions of spirits.

47. VUAL. He first appears in the form of a mighty dromedary; but he puts on human shape at the command of the sorcerer. He speaks the Egyptian tongue, but not perfectly. He procures the love of women, and tells of things past, present, and to come. He also procures friendship between friends and foes. He governs 37 legions of spirits.

48. HAAGENTI. He first appears in the form of a mighty bull with griffin's wings, but puts on human shape at the command of the sorcerer. He makes people wise, and instructs them in diverse things; transmutes all metals into gold; and changes wine into water, and water into wine. He governs 33 legions of spirits.

49. PROCEL or CROCELL. He appears in the form of an angel, speaking mystically of hidden things. He teaches the art of geometry and the liberal sciences. He can reproduce great noises like the running of great waters. He warms waters, and discovers baths. He governs 48 legions of spirits.

50. FURCAS. He appears in the form of a cruel old human with a long beard and a hairy head, sitting on a pale-colored horse, with a sharp weapon in his hand. He teaches the arts of philosophy, astrology, rhetoric, logic, chiromancy, and pyromancy. He governs 20 legions of spirits.

51. BALAM. He appears with three heads: the first like a bull's, the second like a human's, and the third like a ram's. He has a serpent's tail, and flaming eyes. He rides upon a furious bear, and carries a goshawk on his fist. He speaks with a hoarse voice, giving true answers of things past, present, and to come. He can make people invisible and witty. He governs 40 legions of spirits.

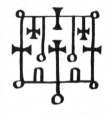

52. ALLOCES. He appears in the form of a soldier riding upon a great horse. His face appears like a lion's, very red, and having flaming eyes. He speaks with a hoarse and loud voice. He teaches the art of astronomy and all the liberal sciences. He brings good familiars. He governs 36 legions of spirits.

53. CAIM or CAMIO. He appears at first in the form of a thrush; but at the command of the sorcerer, he puts on the shape of a human carrying in his hand a sharp sword. He seems to answer in burning ashes. He gives the understanding of all birds, lowing of bullocks, barking of dogs, and other creatures; and also the noise of the waters. He causes disputes. He gives true answers of things to come. He governs 30 legions of spirits.

54. MURMUR or MURMUS. He appears in the form of a soldier riding upon a griffin and wearing a duke's crown. Two of his ministers go before him with great trumpets sounding. He teaches philosophy, and constrains deceased souls to come before the sorcerer to answer questions. He governs 30 legions of spirits.

55. OROBAS. He appears at first like a horse, but puts on human shape at the command of the sorcerer. He discovers all things past, present, and to come; also gives dignities and prelacies, and the favor of friends and of foes. He gives true answers of divinity and of the creation of the world. He governs 20 legions of spirits.

56. GEMORY. She appears in the form of a beautiful woman wearing a duchess's crown, riding on a great camel. She tells of all things past, present, and to come; reveals hidden treasures; and procures the love of women. She governs 26 legions of spirits.

57. OSE or OSO. He appears at first like a leopard, but puts on human shape at the command of the sorcerer. He makes people cunning in the liberal sciences, and gives true answers of divine and secret things. He also changes a person into any shape that the sorcerer desires, and the person so changed will think like the creature or thing that he changed into. He governs 30 legions of spirits.

58. AMY. He appears at first in the form of a flaming fire, but puts on human shape at the command of the sorcerer. He makes one knowing in astrology and all the liberal sciences. He gives good familiars and can bewray treasure kept by spirits. He governs 36 legions of spirits.

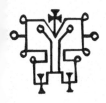

59. ORIAS. He appears in the form of a lion riding upon a mighty horse, with a serpent's tail and holding in his right hand two great serpents hissing. He teaches the virtues of the stars, and knows the mansions of the planets. He transforms people, and gives dignities and prelacies, and confirmations. He also gives favor of friends and foes. He governs 30 legions of spirits.

60. VAPULA. He appears in the form of a lion with griffin's wings. He makes people knowing in all handcrafts and professions, and also philosophy and other sciences. He governs 36 legions of spirits.

61. ZAGAN. He appears at first in the form of a bull with griffin's wings, but puts on human shape at the command of the sorcerer. He makes people witty. He can turn wine into water, blood into wine, and water into wine. He can turn all metals into coin of the country of their origin, and can make fools wise. He governs 33 legions of spirits.

62. VALAK or VOLAC. He appears like a child with angel's wings, riding on a two-headed dragon. He gives true answers of hidden treasures, and tells where to find serpents, which he will bring to the sorcerer without any force or strength. He governs 38 legions of spirits.

63. ANDRAS. He appears in the form of an angel with a head like a night black raven, riding upon a strong black wolf, and flourishing a sharp bright sword. He sows discords. He governs 30 legions of spirits.

64. FLAUROS or HAURES. He appears at first like a mighty, terrible, and strong leopard; but at the command of the sorcerer, he puts on human shape, with fiery eyes and a terrible countenance. He gives true answers of all things present, past, and to come. He will talk of the creation of the world, and of divinity. He destroys and burns the sorcerer's enemies. He governs 36 legions of spirits.

65. ANDREALPHUS. He appears at first in the form of a peacock, with great noises; but he puts on human shape at the command of the sorcerer. He can teach geometry and all things pertaining to measuring, and also astronomy. He can transform a person into the likeness of a bird. He governs 30 legions of spirits.

66. CIMEIES. He appears as a valiant soldier riding upon a goodly black horse. He teaches grammar, logic, and rhetoric; and discovers lost things or hidden treasures. He can make people seem like a soldier in his own likeness. He governs 20 legions of spirits.

67. AMDUSCIAS. He appears at first like a unicorn; but at the command of the sorcerer he puts on human shape, accompanied by trumpets and all manner of musical instruments heard but not seen. He causes trees to bend and incline according to the sorcerer's will. He gives excellent familiars. He governs 29 legions of spirits.

68. BELIAL. He appears in the form of a beautiful angel sitting in a chariot of fire, speaking with a comely voice. He distributes preferments, senatorships, and causes favor of friends and foes. He gives excellent familiars. He governs 80 legions of spirits.

69. DECARABIA. He appears in the form of a star in a pentacle, but puts on human shape at the command of the sorcerer. He discovers the virtues of birds and precious stones, and makes the similitude of all kinds of birds to fly before the sorcerer, singing and drinking as natural birds do. He governs 30 legions of spirits.

70. SEERE or SEER. He appears in the form of a beautiful human, riding upon a strong horse with wings. He brings all things to pass on a sudden, and carries anything where you want it to go. He can pass over the whole world in the twinkling of an eye. He gives a true relation of all sorts of theft, of hidden treasure, and of all other things. He governs 26 legions of spirits.

71. DANTALION. He appears in the form of a human with many faces, all like men's and women's, and has a book in his right hand. He teaches all arts and sciences; and declares the secret counsel of any one; for he knows the thoughts of all men and women, and can change them at his will. He can cause love, and show the similitude of any person, and show the same by a vision, in any part of the world. He governs 36 legions of spirits.

72. ANDROMALIUS. He appears in the form of a human holding a serpent in his hand. He brings back thieves and the stolen goods; discovers all wickedness, and understands dealings; and punishes thieves and other wicked people; and discovers hidden treasures. He governs 36 legions of spirits.

A Goetic Lexicon

artificer—*A skilled or artistic worker or craftsman; one that contrives, devises, or constructs.*

bewray—*Divulge; betray.*

bullock—*A young or castrated bull.*

countenance—*Bearing; demeanor; expression.*

chiromancy—*Palmistry.*

dignity—*Worth, honor, or esteem; high rank, office, or position.*

discord—*Strife; quarreling; conflict.*

distemper—*Bad humor or temper; ailment, disorder.*

goshawk—*A hawk of the northern parts of the Old and the New World that has a white stripe above and behind the eye.*

griffin—*A mythical animal with the head, forepart, and wings of an eagle and the body, hind legs, and tail of a lion.*

hart—*A male red deer; stag.*

liberal arts/sciences—*In classical antiquity, the seven liberal arts consist of rhetoric, logic, grammar, arithmetic, geometry, music, and astronomy.*

phoenix—*A legendary fire-plumed bird that burned itself to ashes, then resurrected itself from those ashes.*

prelacy—*The office or dignity of a prelate (a church office of high rank); priority; seniority.*

pyromancy—*Divination by means of fire or flames.*

rhetoric—*The art of speaking or writing effectively; skill in the effective use of speech.*

senatorship—*A political or governmental position; a member of a senate.*

sepulcher—*Tomb; a receptacle for religious relics, especially in an altar.*

similitude—*Counterpart; double; image; likeness.*

stock-dove—*A dove kept for breeding purposes.*

virtue—*Morality; valor; merit; potency.*

xenophilus—*Definition unknown; some texts use cynocephalus, a dog-headed ape found in the Fortune trump of the tarot.*

CHAPTER FIVE

The Watchtower System

INTRODUCTION

Between 1581 and 1589, Elizabethan magus Dr. John Dee and his seer Edward Kelly received one of the most powerful systems of magick in Western Esotericism. Through communication with numerous entities they called angels, Dee and Kelly assembled a complicated and sometimes contradictory corpus of information on how to understand and control the Elemental forces of nature. They called this system of magick the Enochian system, named after the first Biblical prophet to appear after the great flood.

Of the vast but incomplete collection of Dee's notes that survived his death, two documents have received special attention, mostly due to the efforts of the Hermetic Order of the Golden Dawn to create a viable system from Dee and Kelly's work. The first document, "The Forty-Eight Angelic Keys," contains a collection of nineteen orations transcribed in the Enochian language along with their English translations. These orations work as keys to open the doors to the Elemental realms of the Enochian system.

The second document, "The Book of Supplications and Invocations," begins with the Corrected Great Table, from which

they derive the four Elemental Watchtowers and the Tablet of
Union. The document lists the names and hierarchy of the entities
connected with the Watchtowers and gives some general ideas of
their functions. Together, these two core documents comprise a
vast grimoire of entities with whom to interact.

The original Enochian system possesses a great deal of
power, but it also has many flaws. Dee received and interpreted
the information with an archaic Christian symbolism and
nomenclature, an element of his personal paradigm and not an
integral part of the Enochian system. The entities named upon
the tablets appear and behave as spiritual entities that govern the
forces of nature; they do not act like angels in the Qabalistic or
Christian systems. Furthermore, the Christian paradigm and its
inherent sexism do not resonate well with many modern magicians,
and diminishes the effectiveness of the Enochian system.

The original Enochian system also lacks consistent symmetry.
Some parts of the system defy the logical symmetry inherent in
the rest of the system. For example, Dee breaks the four Greater
Names of Power that govern the Watchtowers into groups of
three, four, and five letters (ORO IBAH AOZPI), and many
Enochian practitioners have struggled to explain the arrangement.
When you put the Greater Names of Power in their proper
astrological context, you realize that they represent the expression
of the zodiac through the four Elements, and that you should
vibrate them as one unbroken name (OROIBAHAOZPI).

Traditional Enochian scholars invariably seek to solve
these problems by looking back into the past, poring through
incomplete notes for answers, writing obscure papers to justify
idiosyncrasies in the system, and attempting to perform the
Enochian rituals exactly as Dee and Kelly did over 400 years ago.

I have chosen to move forward using the spiritual technology of the New Aeon to repair, streamline and strengthen the system. I call it the Watchtower system to distinguish it from the original Enochian system.

The Watchtower system redevelops the two traditional Enochian documents into a complete and workable system of evocation. I replaced the Christian paradigm with one suggested by the Enochian entities themselves, a metaphorical paradigm revealed to Dee & Kelly: a conceptual representation of the terrestrial universe as a great city. The four Elemental Watchtowers administrate this city, and the Palace of Spirit in the center governs the Watchtowers. The various entities of the Watchtowers make up the citizens of this city, representing the different Elemental forces that make up the terrestrial universe. I changed the titles of the Watchtower entities to reflect this paradigm, but their Enochian names and characteristics remain intact.

I retranslated the Nineteen Keys, changing the references to a Christian god to make them gender-neutral and atheistic; I have listed the Enochian words and their Watchtower retranslations in Appendix 1. Appendix 2 documents the changes I made to the original Enochian system. I have also included a version of the Opening by Watchtower revised to reflect these changes in Appendix 3. Finally, Appendix 4 presents a transcription of a Watchtower evocation that I performed some years ago.

I have successfully worked with the Watchtower System for many years, and I encourage you to experiment with this system and discover the power and wonder that it holds. The entities within this grimoire can help you understand the complex Elemental structure within you as well as the Elemental world around you. A vast realm of new entities and experiences await!

HIERARCHY OF THE WATCHTOWER ENTITIES

The entities of the Watchtower System function within in a hierarchical structure. As you progress downward within the hierarchy, the entities become more specific and more limited in their powers.

Names of Power

Names of Power represent spiritual forces or energies that empower the various entities of the Watchtower system. Vibrate the Names of Power before summoning the entities to appear or otherwise employing them. Think of the two parts in terms of force and form, where both parts must work together to achieve manifestation.

The Palace of Spirit

The four rows of the Palace of Spirit give the names of the Elder Spirits of the Elements. The first column of the Palace of Spirit, EHNB, represents the Elder Spirit of Spirit, the highest entity in the hierarchy of the Watchtower System. The remaining four columns of the Palace of Spirit give the Supreme Names of Power, which we never directly evoke.

E	X	A	R	P
H	C	O	M	A
N	A	N	T	A
B	I	T	O	M

ELDER	Elemental Attribution
EHNB	Spirit of Spirit
EXARP	Spirit of Air
HCOMA	Spirit of Water
NANTA	Spirit of Earth
BITOM	Spirit of Fire

Watchtower Crosses and Names of Power

A large white cross, known as the Greater Cross, separates each Watchtower into four Elemental Quarters. The horizontal bar of the Greater Cross gives the Greater Name of Power. The Elemental Quarters contain smaller white crosses called Lesser Crosses, which give the two Lesser Names of Power.

R	Z	I	L	A	F	A	Y	T	L	P	A
A	R	D	Z	A	I	D	P	A	L	A	M
C	Z	O	N	S	A	R	O	Y	A	V	B
T	O	I	T	T	Z	O	P	A	C	O	C
S	I	G	A	S	O	M	R	B	Z	N	H
F	M	O	N	D	A	T	D	I	A	R	I
O	R	O	I	B	A	H	A	O	Z	P	I
T	N	A	B	R	V	I	X	G	A	S	D
O	I	I	I	T	T	P	A	L	O	A	I
A	B	A	M	O	O	O	A	C	U	C	A
N	A	O	C	O	T	T	N	P	R	N	T
O	C	A	N	M	A	G	O	T	R	O	I
S	H	I	A	L	R	A	P	M	Z	O	X

Greater Name of Power	Elemental Attribution
OROIBAHAOZPI	Air

Lesser Names of Power	Elemental Quarter
IDOIGO & ARDZA	Air of Air
LLACZA & PALAM	Water of Air
AIAOAI & OIIIT	Earth of Air
AOURRZ & ALOAI	Fire of Air

Watchtower Entities

I. **Greater Name of Power.** A name of twelve letters representing the twelve signs of the zodiac acting through the Elements. Evoke these names in all Watchtower workings.

R	Z	I	L	A	F	A	Y	T	L	P	A
A	R	D	Z	A	I	D	P	A	L	A	M
C	Z	O	N	S	A	R	O	Y	A	V	B
T	O	I	T	T	Z	O	P	A	C	O	C
S	I	G	A	S	O	M	R	B	Z	N	H
F	M	O	N	D	A	T	D	I	A	R	I
O	R	O	I	B	A	H	A	O	Z	P	I
T	N	A	B	R	V	I	X	G	A	S	D
O	I	I	I	T	T	P	A	L	O	A	I
A	B	A	M	O	O	O	A	C	U	C	A
N	A	O	C	O	T	T	N	P	R	N	T
O	C	A	N	M	A	G	O	T	R	O	I
S	H	I	A	L	R	A	P	M	Z	O	X

Greater Name of Power of Air: OROIBAHAOZPI

Greater Names of Power	Elemental Attribution
OROIBAHAOZPI	Zodiac of Air
MPHARSLGAIOL	Zodiac of Water
MORDIALHCTGA	Zodiac of Earth
OIPTEAAPDOCE	Zodiac of Fire

2. Elemental King. (Spiral of eight letters in the center of the Watchtower.) The Elemental Kings represent the Solar ministers of the Greater Names of Power. Evoke the Elemental Kings in all Watchtower workings in order to access the energy of the Greater Name of Power.

R	Z	I	L	A	F	A	Y	T	L	P	A
A	R	D	Z	A	I	D	P	A	L	A	M
C	Z	O	N	S	A	R	O	Y	A	V	B
T	O	I	T	T	Z	O	P	A	C	O	C
S	I	G	A	S	O	M	R	B	Z	N	H
F	M	O	N	D	A	T	D	I	A	R	I
O	R	O	I	B	A	H	A	O	Z	P	I
T	N	A	B	R	V	I	X	G	A	S	D
O	I	I	I	T	T	P	A	L	O	A	I
A	B	A	M	O	O	O	A	C	U	C	A
N	A	O	C	O	T	T	N	P	R	N	T
O	C	A	N	M	A	G	O	T	R	O	I
S	H	I	A	L	R	A	P	M	Z	O	X

Elemental King of Air: BATAIVAH

Elemental Kings	Elemental Attribution
BATAIVAH	Sol of Air
RAAGIOSL	Sol of Water
ICZHIHAL	Sol of Earth
ELDPRNAA	Sol of Fire

3. Six Seniors. (Six names of seven letters derived from the Greater Cross, beginning in the center and radiating outward.) The Seniors represent the energies of the planets as expressed through the Elements.

R	Z	I	L	A	F	A	Y	T	L	P	A
A	R	D	Z	A	I	D	P	A	L	A	M
C	Z	O	N	S	A	R	O	Y	A	V	B
T	O	I	T	T	Z	O	P	A	C	O	C
S	I	G	A	S	O	M	R	B	Z	N	H
F	M	O	N	D	A	T	D	I	A	R	I
O	R	O	I	B	A	H	A	O	Z	P	I
T	N	A	B	R	V	I	X	G	A	S	D
O	I	I	I	T	T	P	A	L	O	A	I
A	B	A	M	O	O	O	A	C	U	C	A
N	A	O	C	O	T	T	N	P	R	N	T
O	C	A	N	M	A	G	O	T	R	O	I
S	H	I	A	L	R	A	P	M	Z	O	X

Seniors	Elemental Attribution
HABIORO	Mars of Air
AAOZAIF	Jupiter of Air
HTMORDA	Mercury of Air
AHAOZPI	Venus of Air
HIPOTGA	Saturn of Air
AVTOTAR	Luna of Air

Entities of the Elemental Quarters

4. Four Wardens. (Permutations of four letters above the Lesser crossbar.)

Activate each Warden using a Kerubic Name of Power. (First letter from the Spirit of the Element + four letters above the Lesser crossbar.)

E	T	N	A	B	R
	O	I	I	I	T
X	A	B	A	M	O
A	N	A	O	C	O
R	O	C	A	N	M
P	S	H	I	A	L

Wardens	Elemental Attribution
ETNBR	Earth of Air (Kerubic Name of Power)
TNBR	(Air of Earth) of Air
NBRT	(Water of Earth) of Air
BRTN	(Earth of Earth) of Air
RTNB	(Fire of Earth) of Air

5. Four Masters. (Four rows under the Lesser crossbar.) Activate each Master using the corresponding pair of Lesser Names of Power from crossbar.

T	N	A	B	R
O	I	I	I	T
A	B	A	M	O
N	A	O	C	O
O	C	A	N	M
S	H	I	A	L

Masters	Elemental Attribution
AIAOAI & OIIIT	Earth of Air (Lesser Names of Power)
ABMO	(Air of Earth) of Air
NACO	(Water of Earth) of Air
OCNM	(Earth of Earth) of Air
SHAL	(Fire of Earth) of Air

6. Eight Children. (One letter from the Spirit of the Element + two letters below the Lesser crossbar.) Activate the Children using the two Reversed Lesser Names of Power. Always evoke the Children in pairs.

E	T	N	A	B	R
	O	I	I	I	T
X	A	B	A	M	O
A	N	A	O	C	O
R	O	C	A	N	M
P	S	H	I	A	L

Children	Elemental Attribution
IAOAIA & TIIIO	Earth of Air (Reversed Lesser Names of Power)
XAB & XMO	(Air of Earth) of Air
ANA & ACO	(Water of Earth) of Air
ROC & RNM	(Earth of Earth) of Air
PSH & PAL	(Fire of Earth) of Air

WATCHTOWER EVOCATION

Selecting an Entity to Evoke

Entities of the Watchtower system have almost no objective identity, which may make it difficult to decide who to talk to. For this reason, I strongly suggest that you perform exploratory evocations before getting into results-oriented operations. If you want to know anything about an entity or what services it performs, call it up and ask!

The five Elements provide the primary objective framework for understanding the entities Watchtower system. You must have practical experience working with the five Elements before evoking Watchtower entities, knowing not just the Elemental names and attributions, but also how the different Elemental energies feel and move. You'll find many excellent books on the shelf that teach Elemental magick; I recommend the Elemental exercises presented in *Modern Magick* by Donald Michael Kraig.[15]

The Tarot makes a great tool for exploring and understanding the Elements. The four suits of the tarot correspond with the four Elements, and you can find many Elemental interactions within the trumps. The sixteen court cards correspond with the sixteen sub-Elements (Fire of Fire, Fire of Water, etc.), which makes them useful tools for understanding the Elemental Quarters of the Watchtowers. Reading tarot reveals how the five Elements work together in different ways on the Material plane.

If you have not performed Enochian or Watchtower workings before, start with evoking the Elemental Kings and Planetary Seniors of the Watchtowers. They will give you advice on how to best employ the various entities beneath them in the hierarchy.

---

15   Kraig, *Modern Magick*, Lessons 3–6.

Remember that Watchtower entities become more specific and more limited in their powers as you move further down the hierarchy.

You may also select entities by working out the issue that you wish to address into its most important Elemental parts, and then look for an entity that best represents that combination of Elements. For example, when seeking help with heartburn and acid reflux, I chose the Element of Fire to represent process of digestion and the Element of Water to represent the stomach acids (fluids) out of balance. I evoked XPCN, Warden of the Fire Quarter of the Watchtower of Water, to assist me, and promptly received the proper advice and medical care to remedy the situation.

Temple Setup

Watchtower operations require a skrying medium and a set of five Watchtower Tablets. You may reproduce and enlarge the tablets given in the next section for use in your own operations. I encourage you to make your own set of tablets and add Elemental colors to make them appear more vibrant and energetic.

Arrange the Watchtower tablets in the quarters, placing the Palace of Spirit in the center of the circle. You may also place representatives of the Four Elements in the quarters, such as Elemental Weapons or the Sigils of the Elemental Kings. If you employ a separate seer, they should sit facing the appropriate Watchtower.

You do not need a protective circle or Triangle. Watchtower entities represent Elemental phenomena that we live and interact with on a daily basis. You do not need to protect yourself from them, and you cannot restrain or control them. In any case, I have never encountered nor heard of a malignant Watchtower entity.

The Opening

Begin by performing the Watchtower Pentagram Ritual (WPR). This ritual raises the four Watchtowers in the quarters with the Magician at the center, and it identifies the Magician with the Palace of Spirit. The Opening by Watchtower also achieves this effect.

Stand facing the appropriate Elemental quarter, and read or chant the Keys. Page 100 lists the Keys and their Elemental correspondences. Read the Keys in Enochian; you can read the English translations in addition to the Enochian, but not in place of it.

The weird strings of consonants and vowels that comprise Enochian words may seem very difficult to pronounce. The pronunciation of the Keys does not seem to matter very much, so don't worry if you trip over your own tongue. Intent seems to matter as much as pronunciation.

For those interested in the John Dee's pronunciation of Enochian, I highly recommend the Angelical Psalter in volume one of *The Angelical Language* by Aaron Leitch.[16] Avoid the Golden Dawn method of pronunciation; it uses a spurious correspondence with Hebrew letters to determine the pronunciation of each Enochian letter, resulting in an unnecessarily long string of syllables that dilutes the potency of the Enochian tongue.

---

16   Aaron Leitch, *The Angelical Language: The Complete History and Mythos of the Tongue of the Angels* (Woodbury, MN: Llewellyn, 2010), 237-279.

The Conjuration

You do not need to repeat the Greater Names of Power and the names of the Elemental Kings in the Conjuration, as you have already evoked them in the WPR.

Zacar od zamran, gah (name of entity)!
Odo cicle qaa od zorge!
Dooiap (names of entities in the hierarchy), od _____,
od _____, od _____, od _____, od
_____.

Zacar od zamran, gah (name of entity)!

Translation:

Move and appear, spirit_____!
Open the mysteries of creation and act friendly unto me!
In the name of _____, and...
Move and appear, spirit_____!

Include the names of entities in the hierarchy above the entity you wish to evoke within the conjuration as follows:

- **Elders, Kings, and Seniors:** No additional names needed.
- **Wardens:** Include the names of the King, Seniors, and Kerubic Names of Power in the hierarchy.
- **Masters:** Include the names of the King, Seniors, and Lesser Names of Power in the hierarchy.
- **Children:** Include the names of the King, Seniors, Reversed Lesser Names of Power, and the names of both Children in the hierarchy.

For added effect, you may trace the names of the entities on the Watchtowers as you vibrate them.

The Reception

When you make contact and obtain a vision, test the entity by vibrating its name. You may also use other means to verify the identity of the entity, such as giving the Elemental Signs or making Elemental pentagrams. Once you have completed the verification, welcome the entity and thank it for coming. Treat Watchtower entities in a friendly and respectful manner; do not command or threaten them like Goetic spirits. You need not ask entities to swear to an Oath, for they always speak the truth as they understand it and never act in a malevolent manner.

While the Ancient Greeks and Romans often associated Elementals with specific locations on the Material plane, Watchtower entities do not correspond with specific physical locations. They represent various Elemental forces and phenomena within the natural world, but from a much different perspective or paradigm. As a result, Watchtower entities may have an unusual or even alien appearance in visions. They may take humanoid forms, or they may appear as animals, fish, or geometric shapes. Sometimes they appear as a natural phenomenon that corresponds with their Elemental makeup: mountains, bodies of water, volcanoes, etc.

The Interview and Charge

Initial conversations with Watchtower entities usually start with an interview. You know very little about the entity before you, so begin by getting to know them better. Ask them what physical phenomena they govern or rule over. You can also ask them about other Watchtower entities above or below them in the hierarchy; they often offer interesting perspectives about other parts of the system. Ask questions! If entities do not want to answer, they will politely let you know.

Once you have some familiarity with the entity, inquire as to what services it can perform for you. If you decide to call upon it for help, ask it to explain how it will accomplish the task. Watchtower entities sometimes have trouble understanding the way things work on the Material Plane, so attempt to determine if the entity will turn your life upside-down while completing a service. You may want to consider consulting a third party for advice, such as your personal Daemon or a tarot deck. Always remember that you have no obligation to accept help from the entity.

The Dismissal

When you have finished conversing with the entity, thank it for coming and give it license to depart. Then use the WPR or Greater Ritual of the Pentagram to disperse any unbalanced Elemental energies that may linger from the evocation. Close the temple as you see fit, and make sure to ground yourself after the operation.

THE WATCHTOWER
PENTAGRAM RITUAL

1. Stand in the center of the circle, facing East.
   Vibrate *EXARP. HCOMA. NANTA. BITOM.*

2. Clasp your hands upon your breast and vibrate *EHNB.*

3. Move to the East and trace the invoking pentagram of Active
   Spirit, vibrating *EXARP.*
   Trace the Invoking Pentagram of Air, vibrating
   OROIBAHAOZPI.
   Draw King sigil (T with four Yods), vibrating *BATAIVAH.*
   Salute with Air Sign.

4. Move to the West and trace the invoking pentagram of Passive
   Spirit, vibrating *HCOMA.*
   Trace the invoking pentagram of Water, vibrating
   MPHARSLGIAOL.
   Draw King sigil (Cross with b 4 6 b), vibrating *RAAGIOSL.*
   Salute with Water Sign.

5. Move to the North and trace the invoking pentagram of
   Passive Spirit, vibrating *NANTA.*
   Trace the invoking pentagram of Earth, vibrating
   MORDIALHCTGA.
   Draw King sigil (Cross of Elements), vibrating *ICZHIHAL.*
   Salute with Earth Sign.

6. Move to the South trace the invoking pentagram of Active
Spirit, vibrating **BITOM.**
Trace the invoking pentagram of Fire, vibrating
OIPTEAAPDOCE.
Draw King sigil (Sun of 12 rays), vibrating **ELDPRNAA.**
Salute with Fire Sign.

7. Complete the circle and return to the center.

8. Say "For about me stand the Watchtowers, and within
me stands the Palace of Spirit."

9. Repeat the Column of Spirit (parts 1-2).

ICZHIHAL

RAAGIOSL   BATAIVAH

ELDPRNAA

THE EIGHTEEN KEYS

Key Attributions

Select the Keys appropriate for each entity as follows:

EHNB: First and Second Key.
Elder Spirits of the Elements: First Key.
Kings & Seniors: Elemental Key (3-6).
Wardens, Masters, and Children: Elemental Key (3-6),
Sub-Elemental Key (7-18) that corresponds to the
Elemental Quarter.

Elemental Correspondences

1. Spirit (Palace)
2. Spirit (EHNB)

3. Air, Air of Air
4. Water, Water of Water
5. Earth, Earth of Earth
6. Fire, Fire of Fire

7. Water of Air
8. Earth of Air
9. Fire of Air

10. Air of Water
11. Earth of Water
12. Fire of Water

13. Air of Earth
14. Water of Earth
15. Fire of Earth

16. Air of Fire
17. Water of Fire
18. Earth of Fire

The First Key

Ol sonf vorsg, goho iad balt, lansh calz vonpho; Sobra zol ror i ta nazpsad, graa ta malprg; Ds holq qaa nothoa zimz, od commah ta nobloh zien; Soba thil gnonp prge aldi; ds urbs oboleh grsam; Casarm ohorela caba Pir; Ds zonrensg cab erm iadnah. Pilah farzm znrza adna gono iadpil, ds hom toh; Soba ipam, ul ipamis; Ds loholo vep zomdux poamal, od bogpa aai ta piap baltle od vooan. Zacar, ca, od zamran; odo cicle qaa; zorge, lap zirdo noco mad, hoath iaida.

I reign over you, says the unity of justice, in power exalted above the firmaments of wrath; in whose hands the sun is as a sword, and the moon a penetrating fire; Who measures your garments in the midst of my vestures, and trussed you together as the palms of my hands; Whose seats I garnished with the fire of gathering, and beautified your garments with admiration; to Whom I made a law to govern the holy ones, and delivered you a rod with the ark of knowledge. Moreover, you lifted up your voices and swore obedience and faith to unity triumphant; whose beginning is not, nor end cannot be; which shines as a flame in the midst of your palace, and reigns among you as the balance of righteousness and truth. Move, therefore, and show yourselves; open the mysteries of your creation; be friendly unto me; for I am the servant of truth, the true worshipper of the highest unity.

The Second Key

Adgt upaah zong om faaip sald, viiv L? Sobam ialprg izazaz piadph; Casarma abramg ta talho paracleda, qta lorlsq turbs ooge baltoh. Givi chis lusd orri od micalp chis bia ozongon; lap noan trof cors tage oq manin iaidon. Torzu, gohel: zacar, ca, cnoqod; zamran micalzo, od ozazm urelp; lap zir ioiad.

Can the wings of the winds understand your voices of wonder, o you the second of the First? Whom the burning flames have framed within the depths of my jaws; Whom I have prepared as cups for a wedding, or as the flowers in their beauty for the chamber of righteousness. Stronger are your feet than the barren stone and mightier are your voices than the manifold winds; for you are become a building such as is not but in the mind of unity. Arise, says the First; move, therefore, unto his servants; show yourselves in power, and make me a strong seething; for I am of eternity.

The Third Key

Micma, goho piad, zir comselh azien bia oslondoh. Norz chis othil gigipah undl chis tapuin, qmospleh teloch, quiin toltorg chis ichisge, m ozien, dst brgda od torzul. Ili eol balzarg od aala thilnos netaab, dluga vomsarg lonsa capmiali vors cla, homil cocasb fafen izizop od miinoag de gnetaab vaun nanaeel, panpir malpirgi caosg pild. Noan unalah balt odvooan. Dooiap mad, goholor, gohus, amiran. Micma iehusoz cacacom od dooain noar micaolz aaiom. Casarmg gohia: Zacar, uniglag, od imvamar pugo plapli ananael qaan.

Behold, says the unity of all, I am a circle on whose hands stand twelve kingdoms. Six are the seats of the living breath, the rest are as sharp sickles or the horns of death, wherein the creatures of the earth are, and are not, except by my own hand, which sleep and shall rise. In the first I made you stewards and placed you in seats twelve of government, giving unto every one of you power successively over 456, the true ages of time, to the intent that from the highest vessels and corners of your governments you might work my power, pouring down the fires of life and increase on the earth continually. Thus you are become the skirts of justice and truth. In the name of truth, lift up, I say, yourselves. Behold the mercies that flourish and the name is become mighty among us. In whom we say: Move, descend, and apply yourselves unto us as partakers of the secret wisdom of creation.

The Fourth Key

Othil lasdi babage od dorpha gohol; gchisge avavago cormp pd, dsonf vivdiv? Casarmi oali mapm, sobam ag cormpo crpl. Casarmg croodzi chis odugeg; dst capimali, chis capimaon; odlonshin chis talo cla. Torgu, norquasahi, od fcaosga; bagle zirenaiad dsi odapila. Dooiap qaal, zacar, odzamran obelisong, restil aaf normolap.

I have set my feet in the south and have looked about me saying: are not the thunders of increase numbered 33, which reign in the second angle? Under whom I have placed 9639 whom none has yet numbered but one. In whom the second beginning of things are and wax strong; which also successively are the number of time; and their powers are as the first 456. Arise, you children of pleasure, and visit the earth; for I am the cosmic union which is and lives. In the name of creation, move, and show yourselves as pleasant deliverers, that you may praise me among the children of humanity.

The Fifth Key

Sapah zimii duiv od noas taqanis adroch, dorphal caosg od faonts piripsol tablior, casarm amipzi nazarth af, od dlugar zizop zlida caosgi toltorgi; od zchis esiasch l taviv, od iaod thild ds hubar peral, soba cormfa chista la, uls, od qcocash. Ca niis od darbs qaas; fetharzi od bliora; iaial ednas cicles, bagle geiadil.

The mighty sounds have entered in the third angle and are become as olives on the tree looking with gladness upon the earth and dwelling in the brightness of the heavens as comforters, unto whom I fastened pillars of gladness nineteen, and gave them vessels to water the earth with all her creatures; and they are the kin of the first and second, and the beginning of their own seats, which are garnished with continual burning lamps 69636, whose numbers are as the first, the end, and the content of time. Therefore come and obey your creation; visit us in peace and comfort; include us as receivers of your mysteries, for our unity is one.

The Sixth Key

Gah sdiv chisem, micalzo pilzin; sobam el harg mir babalon od obloc samvelg, dlugar malpurg arcaosgi, od acam canal sobolzar fbliard caosgi, odchis anetab od miam taviv od d. Darsar, solpeth bien; brita od zacam gmicalzo, sobhaath trian luiahe odecrin mad qaaon.

The spirits of the fourth angle are nine, mighty in the firmament of waters; whom the first has planted a torment to the wicked and a garland to the righteous, giving unto them fiery darts to winnow the earth, and 7699 continual workers whose courses visit with comfort the earth; and are in government and continuance as the second and the third. Wherefore, harken unto my voice; I have talked of you and I move you in power and presence, you whose works shall be a song of honor and the praise of truth in creation.

The Seventh Key

Raas isalman paradiz oecrimi aao ialpirgah; quiin enay butmon, od inoas ni paradial casarmg ugear chirlan, od zonac luciftian corsta vaulzirn tolhami. Soba londoh odmiam chistad odes, umadea od pibliar, othilrit odmiam. Cnoquol rit, zacar, zamran, oecrimi qadah; od omicaolz aaiom; bagle papnor idlugam lonshi, od umplif ugegi bigliad.

The east is a house of virgins singing praises among the flames of first glory; wherein the universe has opened its mouth, and they become 28 living dwellings in whom the strength of humanity rejoices, and they are appareled with ornaments of brightness such as work wonders on all creatures. Whose kingdoms and continuance are as the third and fourth, strong towers and places of comfort, the seats of mercy and continuance. O you servants of mercy, move, appear, sing praises unto creation; and be mighty among us; for to this remembrance is given power, and our strength waxes strong in our comfort.

The Eighth Key

Bazemlo, ita piripson oln nazavabh ox, casarmg uran chis ugeg; dsabramg batloha, gohoiad, solamien train talolcis abaivonin od aziagiar rior. Irgilchisda, dspaaox busd caosgo, dschis odipuran teloah cacrg oisalman loncho od vovina carbaf! Niiso, bagle avavago gohon; niiso, bagle momao siaion, od mabza iadoiasmomar, poilp. Niis, zamran ciaofi caosgo; od bliors; od corsi ta abramig.

The midday, the first, is as the third heaven made of pillars of hyacinth 26, in whom the elders are become strong; which I have prepared for my own righteousness, says the unity of all things; whose long continuance shall be bucklers to the stooping dragon and like unto the harvest of a widow. How many are there, which remain in the glory of the earth, which are and shall not see death until this house fall and the dragon sink! Come away, for the thunders have spoken; come away, for the crowns of the temple, and the coat of the unity that is, was, and shall be crowned, are divided. Come, appear to the terror of the earth; and to our comfort; and of such as are prepared.

The Ninth Key

Micaoli bransg prgel napta ialpor (dsbrin efafafe p vonpho olani od obza; sobca upaah chis tatan od tranan bayle) alar lusda sobon od chisholq cnoquodi cial. Unal aldon mom caosgo ta lasollor gnay limlal. Amma chiis sobca madrid zchis! Ooanoan chis aviny drilpi caosgin, od butmoni parm zumvi cnila: dazis ethamz achildao, od mirc ozol chis pidiai collal. Ulcinin asobam ucim, bagle iadbaltoh chirlan par. Niiso od ip ofafafe! Bagle acocash icorsca unig blior.

A mighty guard of fire with two-edged swords flaming (which have vials eight of wrath for two times and a half, whose wings are of wormwood and of the narrow of salt), have settled their feet in the west and are measured with their ministers 9996. These gather up the moss on the earth as the rich man does his treasure. Cursed are they whose iniquities they are! In their eyes are millstones greater than the earth, and from their mouths rain seas of blood: their heads are covered with diamonds, and upon their hands are marble sleeves. Happy is he on whom they frown not, because the unity of righteousness rejoices in them. Come away and not your vials! For the time is such as requires comfort.

The Tenth Key

Coraxo chis cormp od blans lucal aziazor paeb, soba lilonon chis virq eophan od raclir maasi bagle caosgi; ds ialpon dosig od basgim od oxex dazis siatris od salbrox cinxir faboan. Unalchis const ds daox cocasg ol oanio yor torb vohim gizyax, od matb cocasg plosi molui, ds pageip larag om droln matorb cocasb emna. Lpatralx yolci matb nomig monons olora gnay angelard. Ohio Ohio Ohio Ohio Ohio Ohio, noib, Ohio caosgon, bagle madrid i, zirop, chiso drilpa. Niiso, crip ip nidali.

The thunders of judgment and wrath are numbered and are harbored in the north in the likeness of an oak, whose branches are 22 nests of lamentation and weeping laid up for the earth; which burn night and day and vomit out the heads of scorpions and live sulfur mingled with poison. These are the thunders that 5678 times in the 24th part of a moment roar with a hundred mighty earthquakes, and a thousand times as many surges, which rest not nor know any echoing time here. One rock brings forth a thousand even as the heart of a human does his thoughts. Woe Woe Woe Woe Woe Woe, Yes, Woe be to the earth, for her iniquity is, was, and shall be great. Come away, but not your noises.

The Eleventh Key

Oxiayal holdo od zirom o coraxo ds zildar raasy, od vabzir camilax od bahal: Niiso! Od aldon od noassalman teloch, casarman holq, od ti ta zchis soba cormf iga. Niisa, bagle abramg noncp. Zacar, ca, od zamran; odo cicle qaa; zorge, lap zirdo noco mad, hoath iaida.

The mighty seat groaned and there were five thunders which flew into the east, and the Eagle spake and cried with a loud voice: Come away! And they gathered themselves together and became the house of death, of whom it is measured, and it is as they are whose number is 31. Come away, for I have prepared for you. Move, therefore, and show yourselves; open the mysteries of your creation; be friendly unto me, for I am the servant of truth, the true worshipper of the highest unity.

The Twelfth Key

Nonci dsonf babage od chis ob hubaio tibibp allar, atraah od ef! Drix fafen mian ar enay ovof, Soba dooain aai ivonph. Zacar, gohus, od zamran; odo cicle qaa; zorge, lap zirdo noco mad, hoath iaida.

O you that reign in the south and are 28 the lanterns of sorrow bind up your girdles and visit us! Bring down your followers 3663 that the cosmos may be magnified, whose name among you is wrath. Move, I say, and show yourselves; open the mysteries of your creation; be friendly unto me, for I am the servant of truth, the true worshipper of the highest unity.

The Thirteenth Key

Napeai babagen, dsbrin ux ooaona lring vonph doalim, eolis ollog orsba dschis affa; micma isro mad od lonshitox ds iumd aai grosb; zacar od zamran; odo cicle qaa; zorge, lap zirdo noco mad, hoath iaida.

O you swords of the south, which have 42 eyes to stir up the wrath of sin, making humanity drunken which are empty; behold the promise of truth and the power of virtue which is called among you a bitter sting; move and show yourselves; open the mysteries of your creation; be friendly unto me, for I am the servant of truth, the true worshipper of the highest unity.

The Fourteenth Key

Noromi bagie, pasbs oiad, ds trint mirc ol thil, dods tolham caosgo homin, dsbrin oroch quar; micma bial oiad, aisro tox dsium aai baltim. Zacar od zamran; odo cicle qaa; zorge, lap zirdo noco mad, hoath iaida.

O you sons of fury, the daughters of unity, which sit upon 24 seats, vexing all creatures of the earth with age, which have under you 1636; behold the voice of unity, the promise of virtue which is called among you extreme justice. Move and show yourselves; open the mysteries of your creation; be friendly unto me, for I am the servant of truth, the true worshipper of the highest unity.

The Fifteenth Key

Yls tabaan lialprt, casarman upaahi chis darg, dsoado caosgi orscor, ds omax monasci Baeovib od emetgis iaiadix: zacar od zamran; odo cicle qaa; zorge, lap zirdo noco mad, hoath iaida.

O thou the governor of the first flame, under whose wings are 6379, which weave the earth with dryness, which knows the great name Righteousness and the seal of honor; move and show yourselves; open the mysteries of your creation; be friendly unto me, for I am the servant of truth, the true worshipper of the highest unity.

The Sixteenth Key

Yls vivialprt salman balt ds acroodzi busd od bliorax balit; dsinsi caosg lusdan emod dsom od tliob: drilpa geh yls madzilodarp. Zacar od zamran; odo cicle qaa; zorge, lap zirdo noco mad, hoath iaida.

O thou of the second flame, the house of justice which hast thy beginning in glory and shall comfort the just; who walks on the earth with feet 8763 that understand and separate creatures: great art thou in the truth of dominion. Move and show yourselves; open the mysteries of your creation; be friendly unto me, for I am the servant of truth, the true worshipper of the highest unity.

The Seventeenth Key

Yls dialprt, soba upaah chis nanba zixlay dodsih, odbrint taxs hubaro tastax ylsi; sobaiad ivonpovnph. Aldon daxil od toatar. Zacar od zamran; odo cicle qaa; zorge, lap zirdo noco mad, hoath iaida.

O thou third flame, whose wings are thorns to stir up vexation, and hast 7336 living lamps going before thee, whose union is wrath in anger: gird up thy loins and harken. Move and show yourselves; open the mysteries of your creation; be friendly unto me, for I am the servant of truth, the true worshipper of the highest unity.

The Eighteenth Key

Yls micalzo aipirt ialprg bliors, ds odo busdir oiad ovoars caosgo; casarmg laiad eran brints casasam, ds iumd aqlo adohi moz, od maoffas: bolp comobliort pambt. Zacar od zamran; odo cicle qaa; zorge, lap zirdo noco mad, hoath iaida.

O thou mighty light and burning flame of comfort, which openest the glory of unity to the center of the earth; in whom the secrets of truth 6332 have their abiding, which is called in thy kingdom joy, and not to be measured: be thou a window of comfort unto me. Move and show yourselves; open the mysteries of your creation; be friendly unto me, for I am the servant of truth, the true worshipper of the highest unity.

THE THIRTY AETHYRS AND THE NINETEENTH KEY

The role of the Thirty Aethyrs in the Watchtower System seems unclear. Dee envisioned them as a series of concentric circles with the four Watchtowers placed in the center. In operations dealing with the Thirty Aethyrs, one starts with the innermost ring, TEX, and moves outward to LIL. Read the Nineteenth Key to activate the vision, and vibrate the names of the Governors to test it.

Personal accounts such as Aleister Crowley's *The Vision and the Voice* demonstrate that the use of the Nineteenth Key inspires visions of a highly personal and magical nature. I present the information on the Thirty Aethyrs here to inspire further research.

The Governors of the Thirty Aethyrs

1	LIL	OCCODON, PASCOMB, VALGARS
2	ARN	DOAGNIS, PACASNA, DIALIOA
3	ZOM	SAMAPHA, VIROOLI, ANDISPI
4	PAZ	THOTANP, AXZIARG, POTHNIR
5	LIT	LAZDIXI, NOCAMAL, TIARPAX
6	MAZ	SAXTOMP, VAVAAMP, ZIRZIRD
7	DEO	OPMACAS, GENADOL, ASPIAON
8	ZID	ZAMFRES, TODNAON, PRISTAC
9	ZIP	ODDIORG, CRALPIR, DOANZIN
10	ZAX	LEXARPH, COMANAN, TABITOM
11	ICH	MOLPAND, USNARDA, PONODOL
12	LOE	TAPAMAL, GEDOONS, AMBRIOL
13	ZIM	GECAOND, LAPARIN, DOCEPAX
14	UTA	TEDOOND, VIVIPOS, OOANAMB
15	OXO	TAHAMDO, NOCIABI, TASTOXO
16	LEA	CUCARPT, LAUACON, SOCHIAL
17	TAN	SIGMORF, AVDROPT, TOCARZI
18	ZEN	NABAOMI, ZAFASAI, YALPAMB
19	POP	TORZOXI, ABRIOND, OMAGRAP
20	CHR	ZILDRON, PARZIBA, TOTOCAN
21	ASP	CHIRZPA, TOANTOM, VIXPALG
22	LIN	OZIDAIA, LAZDIXI, CALZIRG
23	TOR	RONOOMB, ONIZIMP, ZAXANIN
24	NIA	ORCANIR, CHALSPO, SOAGEEL
25	UTI	MIRZIND, OBVAORS, RANGLAM
26	DES	POPHAND, NIGRANA, BAZCHIM
27	ZAA	SAZIAMI, MATHULA, ORPANIB
28	BAG	LABNIXP, POCISNI, OXLOPAR
29	RII	VASTRIM, ODRAXTI, GOMZIAM
30	TEX	TAOAGLA, GEMNIMB, ADVORPT, DOXINAL

The Nineteenth Key

Madriax dspraf [name of Aethyr] chismicaolz saanir caosgo, od
fisis balzizras iaida! Nonca gohulim: Micma adoian mad, iaod bliorb;
Sobaooaona chis luciftias piripsol; Ds abraassa noncf netaaib caosgi,
od tilb adphaht damploz; tooat noncf gmicalzoma lrasd tofglo marb
yarry idoigo; od torzulp iaodaf, gohol: caosga, tabaord saanir, od
christeos yrpoil tiobl, busdirtilb noaln paid orsba od dodrmni zilna.
Elzaptilb, parmgi piripsax, od ta qurlst booapis. Lnibm, oucho symp;
od christeos agtoltorn mirc q tiobl lel. Ton paombd, dilzmo aspian, od
christeos agltortorn parach asymp. Cordziz dodpal od fifalz lsmnad;
od fargt, bams omaoas. Conisbra od avavox, tonug. Orscatbl, naosmi
tabges levithmong; unchi omptilb ors. Bagle? Moooah olcordziz.
Lcapimao ixomaxip, odcacocasb gosaa; baglen pii tianta ababalond,
odfaorgt telocvovim. Madriiax, torzu! Oadriax orocha, aboapri.
Tabaori priaz artabas; adrpan corsta dobix. Yolcam priazi arcaozior,
odquasb qting. Ripir paaoxt sagacor; uml od prdzar, cacrg aoiveae
cormpt. Torzu, zacar, odzamran aspt sibsi butmona, ds surzas tia
blatan; odo cicle qaa, od ozazma plapli iadnamad.

O you heavens which dwell in _____ are mighty in the parts of
the earth, and execute the judgment of the highest unity! To you it
is said: Behold the face of truth, the beginning of comfort; whose
eyes are the brightness of the heavens; which provided for you the
government of the earth, and her unspeakable variety; furnishing
you with a power of understanding to dispose all things according
to the providence of existence; and rose up in the beginning, saying:
the earth, let her be governed by her parts, and let there be division
in her, that the glory of her may be always drunken and vexed in
itself. Her course, let it run with the heavens, and as a handmaid let
her serve them. One season, let it confound another, and let there be
no creature upon or within her the same. All her members, let them
differ in their qualities, and let there be no one creature equal with
another. The reasonable creatures of the earth, let them vex and weed
out one another; and the dwelling places, let them forget their names.
The works of humanity and his pomp, let them be defaced. The
buildings, let them become caves for the beasts of the field; confound
her understanding with darkness. Why? I regret that I made
humanity. One while let her be known, and another while a stranger;
because she is the bed of a harlot, and the dwelling place of him
that is fallen. O you heavens, arise! The lower heavens underneath
you, let them serve you. Govern those who govern; cast down such
as fall. Bring forth with those that increase, and destroy the rotten.
No place let it remain in one number; add and diminish, until the
stars be numbered. Arise, move, and appear before the covenant of
the mouth, which has been sworn unto us in infinite justice; open
the mysteries of your creation, and make us partakers of undefiled
knowledge.

APPENDIX I: MODIFICATIONS MADE TO THE ENOCHIAN SYSTEM

• Used Reformed Table as standard, with one letter per square.

• Combined the Three Mystical Names into one name to represent the powers of the zodiac expressed through the Elements.

• Transposed the planetary attributions for Lunar and Mercurial Seniors to preserve planetary balance. (See *Godzilla Meets E.T., Parts 1 & 2* by Benjamin Rowe.)

• Formed the god-name that commands the Wardens (Kerubic Angels) by adding first letter of appropriate Element from Tablet of Union (EHNB).

• Formed the names of the Children (Cacodemons) by adding letter from the appropriate square from Tablet of Union.

• Added children (Cacodemons) from right side of Calvary Cross to form four pairs.

• Changed the names of the Enochian entities in the Elemental Quarters to remove the Christian bias.

• Retranslated terms in the Nineteen Keys to remove the Christian bias and add gender neutrality.

APPENDIX 2: ENOCHIAN-WATCHTOWER TRANSLATIONS

Enochian Word	Key	Dee Translation	Watchtower Translation
Iad (root)	Many	God	Unity, union
Iadpil	1	Him	Unity
Iaidon	2	All Powerful	Unity
Ioiad	2	Him That Liveth Forever	Eternity
Piad	3	God	Unity
Oiad	14, 18	God	Unity
Iaida	Many	Highest	Highest unity
Mad	Many	Your God	Truth
Enay	4, 7, 12	Lord	Universe, cosmos
Qaal	4	Creator	Creation
Qadah	7	Creator	Creation
Idoigo	19	Him who sits on the Holy Throne	Existence
Adroch	5	Olive mount	Olive tree
Zilodarp	16	God of Stretch-forth and conquer	Truth of Dominion
Tia	19	He, his	Infinite
Normolap	4	Sons of men	Children of humanity
Ollog	13	Men	Humanity
Tox	13, 14	Him	Virtue

APPENDIX 3: REVISED OPENING BY WATCHTOWER

1. Opening. Knock once. Perform an Elemental banishing or the WPR.

2. Fire. Walk to South. Face Watchtower, wave fire wand once to left, right, and center. Raise wand above head and walk deosil, saying:

"And when, after all the phantoms have vanished, thou shalt see that holy and formless Fire, that fire which darts and flashes through the hidden depths of the universe, hear thou the voice of Fire."

At South, draw circle of gold. Draw (blue) invoking pentagram of Fire, vibrating *"OIPTEAAPDOCE."* Draw sigil of Leo in center. Point to center with wand and vibrate *"ELDPRNAA."* Raise wand, saying:

"In the names and letters of the Great Southern Quadrangle, I invoke ye, ye entities of the Watchtower of the South."

Visualize and feel Fire energy. Replace wand.

3. Water. Walk to West. Face Watchtower, sprinkle water to left, right, and center. Raise cup and walk deosil, saying:

"So therefore first, the priest who governeth the works of Fire must sprinkle with the lustral water of the loud resounding sea."

At West, draw circle of gold. Draw invoking pentagram of Water, vibrating *"MPHARSLGAIOL."* Draw sigil of Scorpio in center. Point to center and vibrate *"RAAGIOSL."* Raise cup, saying:

"In the names and letters of the Great Western Quadrangle, I invoke ye, ye entities of the Watchtower of the West."

Visualize and feel Water energy. Replace cup.

4. Air. Walk to East. Face Watchtower, shake dagger to left, right, and center. Raise dagger and walk deosil, saying:

"Such a Fire existeth, extending through the rushing of Air. Or even a Fire formless, whence cometh the image of a voice. Or even a flashing light, abounding, revolving, whirling forth, crying aloud."

At East, draw golden circle. Draw invoking pentagram of Air, vibrating *"OROIBAHAOZPI."* Draw sigil of Aquarius in center. Point to center and vibrate *"BATAIVAH."* Raise dagger, saying:

"In the names and letters of the Great Eastern Quadrangle, I invoke ye, ye entities of the Watchtower of the East."

Visualize and feel Air energy. Replace dagger.

5. Earth. Walk to North. Face Watchtower, shake pantacle to left, right, and center. Raise pantacle, saying:

"Wholly divisible, yet indivisible, thence abundantly springeth forth the generations of multifarious matter."

At North, draw golden circle. Draw invoking pentagram of Earth, vibrating *"MORDIALHCTGA."* Draw sigil of Taurus in center. Point to center and vibrate *"ICZHIHAL."* Raise pantacle, saying:

"In the names and letters of the Great Northern Quadrangle, I invoke ye, ye entities of the Watchtower of the North."

Visualize and feel Earth energy. Replace pantacle.

6. Spirit. Return to altar, facing East. Over altar and Tablet, make the sign of "The Rending of the Veil." Say:

"OL SONF VORS G GOHO IAD BALT."
Vibrate: *"LEXARPH COMANAN TABITOM."*
Say: *"ZACARE, CA ZACARE OD ZAMRAN."*
"ODO CICLE QAA PIAP PIAMOL OD VOOAN."

Say:

"I invoke ye, ye entities of the celestial spheres, who dwell in the invisible. Ye guard the gates of the universe; guard ye also this mystic sphere. Keep far removed the evil and the unbalanced. Strengthen and inspire me so that I may preserve unsullied this abode of the mysteries of eternity. Make my sphere pure and holy so that I may enter in and partake of the secrets of the light divine."

Sense and balance Elements at center of circle. Move to the Northeast and say:

"The visible Sun dispenses light unto the Earth. Let me therefore form a vortex in this chamber that the invisible Sun of the spirit may shine therein."

Circumambulate three times, making the Sign of the Enterer each time you pass East. Visualize and feel vortex of energy. Return to West of altar facing East. Make the Sign of the Enterer saying:

Holy art Thou, who art the Universe! (SoE)

Holy art Thou, who art in Nature Formed! (SoE)

Holy art Thou, the Vast and the Mighty! (SoE)

Source of Darkness, Source of Light!

Give the Sign of Silence.

Closing By Watchtower

Circumambulate three times counterclockwise, making the Sign of the Enterer each time you pass East. Visualize and feel the vortex of energy dissipate. Perform an Elemental banishing or the WPR. Say:

"I now release any spirits imprisoned by this ceremony. Depart in peace to your abodes and habitations. I declare this temple duly closed."

Knock once.

Notes

Revised Earth oration taken from the Chaldean Oracles, verses 100-101.

Removed "from above" from Northeast oration.

Adoration to the Lord of the Universe modified to make it gender-neutral. Originally published in initiation rituals of the Open Source Order of the Golden Dawn (osogd.org).

Yeheshuah blessing from Closing omitted.

APPENDIX 4:
AN EVOCATION OF RAAGIOSL, THE
ELEMENTAL KING OF WATER

1/15/02, 10:45-11:30 p.m.
[S. was the seer.] Watchtower tablets placed in quarters, center.
Sigil of King placed in West of Temple.

NBRP[17] (standing in place).
Invoked Water in West using MPHARSLGAIOL.
Chanted First Call, Second Call, and Fourth Call.
Conjuration:

> *Zacar od zamran, gah RAAGIOSL!*
> *Odo cicle qaa od zorge!*
> *Zacar od zamran, gah RAAGIOSL!*

I read the conjuration twice, and then something other than the Elemental King showed up. The seer saw an orange, muppet-like frog with eyes on stalks. I tested the spirit by giving the Water sign and vibrating its name three times, and it appeared unaffected. It was very pleasant, yet simplistic and unintelligent. I got the feeling it was incomplete. It only answered one of my questions:

> *That name I that used to invoke Water at the beginning,*
> *MPHARSLGAIOL: what is that to you?*

> *That is a very great thing. That is like the sky. The great sky. He makes us all.*

When I realized that I wasn't going to get anything useful out of this spirit, I dismissed it. I then repeated the process stated

17   The New Banishing Ritual of the Pentagram, available on my website: www.hermetic.com/osiris. The Watchtower Pentagram Ritual replaced the NBRP in later evocations.

above, making two changes: I drew the circle around S. and myself instead of standing in place, and I spoke rather than chanted the calls. After reciting the conjuration twice, RAAGIOSL showed up. I tested her by vibrating her name six times while giving the Water sign.

Please identify yourself.

[She's making a vibration-noise. It's like I am underwater looking up through the water, and there's rain coming down that's making weird sounds that I don't understand.]

I ask that you speak to me and my seer in the English tongue.

He does not know what I say.

Who are you?

I am that which you have called. I am the Queen of the Waters.

What is your role in the Watchtower System?

I guide the chiefs of my kingdom.

I tried calling you before, and I got a different entity. Do you know why that is?

[She's not exactly explaining this in words. She's describing a bubble coming up from the depths of the ocean, and as it came up I saw in it the same entity that we summoned before. The bubble came up and popped up at the top. What you got was a bubble. We got the right thing, just in the wrong form, and it had such limited scope.]

What is necessary to evoke you? Do we need to recite both the First and the Second Calls in addition to the Fourth?

It is only important to bring forth the energies that support us.

Understood. What do you rule over?

The great depths of the soul.

What can you tell me about the Children of the Elemental Quarters?

They fill my oceans with life.

I am trying to understand the scope of your nature. In the Watchtower System, why would I call upon you as opposed to other entities in the system? What is it that you can do?

I provide space and protection for those who dwell within me. I'll give you nourishment if you wish.

What else can you tell me about yourself?

I control the movements of all within my lands.

Even boats?

Yes.

Who is HCOMA to you?

He is the Father that gave us life.

Is there anything that I can do for you?

You can give us praise when you meet the Great Father.[18]

That I will.

I will nurture and sustain you if you wish.

I am interested, but I would like more details as to how you are going to accomplish this, how you are going to nurture me.

[Here's another visual. She thinks that people live in liquid. I see a picture of you with a coating of liquid around you. It's like a tank of water that you're in, but you're here, and then she does what she wants to do to you. She thinks everything is just water anyway.]

---

18   EHNB, The Spirit of Spirit.

RAAGIOSL, I appreciate your offer of nurture and sustenance, but I do not wish to take you up on that offer at this time, simply because I'm afraid of creating more imbalance within myself. But I do promise you that when I am in a better place, I will call upon you again to take advantage of that which you have to offer. And yes, I will speak well of you to the Great Father, and speak well of your name. Do you understand?

Yes. My nurturing will be helping you in the process though.

Just a second. [Quick consultation with the Black Man.[19]] *I appreciate your offer, but I have been instructed that I need to go about this in a different manner this time. Please take no offense.*

None has been taken.

Good. Do you have any other advice for me?

There is nothing else you need from me at this time.

Then I do thank you for coming here before us, RAAGIOSL. Before I dismiss you, if you so desire, speak to my seer.

[Done.][20]

I have one more question for you before you go. What should I do in the future to avoid the problems that I had earlier this evening--that is, getting the incorrect or incomplete entity?

You will know when it is right and wrong.

Like I did this evening.

Yes.

I do thank thee, O RAAGIOSL, for coming here before me and answering my questions in a pleasant manner. Go back unto your abodes, unto the waters from which you came, the waters that are your home. Go back; you are dismissed; go in peace, love and joy.

---

19   One of my spiritual guides at the time.
20   At the end of Watchtower evocations, I give the spirit an opportunity to talk directly to my seer, allowing him to ask for personal advice or assistance. In this case, the seer accepted the offer of nurture and sustenance that I had declined.

[She's gone.]

Closed with NBRP.

Notes:[21] She often paused before speaking.

[RAAGIOSL never manifested visually. It was a woman's voice. I would get images of being under the water, and she was the water.]

In the second evocation, I had to repeat the conjurations.

[I needed it to strengthen the vision. She showed up the first time.]

I could feel the difference the second time, as if the temple became encased in water. I think that is one reason I started to get so cold toward the end of the evocation, because water isn't necessarily warm.

[I had the sensation we were under water.]

I invoked Water right over your head, in front of the central altar. I didn't go to the West to do the invocation.

---

21   My audio recordings of evocations include the discussion and analysis that occurs after the operation.

CHAPTER SIX:

Entities Of The Watchtowers

THE PALACE OF SPIRIT

E	X	A	R	P
H	C	O	M	A
N	A	N	T	A
B	I	T	O	M

ELDER	Elemental Attribution
EHNB	Spirit of Spirit
EXARP	Spirit of Air
HCOMA	Spirit of Water
NANTA	Spirit of Earth
BITOM	Spirit of Fire

WATCHTOWER OF AIR

R	Z	I	L	A	F	A	Y	T	L	P	A
A	R	D	Z	A	I	D	P	A	L	A	M
C	Z	O	N	S	A	R	O	Y	A	V	B
T	O	I	T	T	Z	O	P	A	C	O	C
S	I	G	A	S	O	M	R	B	Z	N	H
F	M	O	N	D	A	T	D	I	A	R	I
O	R	O	I	B	A	H	A	O	Z	P	I
T	N	A	B	R	V	I	X	G	A	S	D
O	I	I	I	T	T	P	A	L	O	A	I
A	B	A	M	O	O	O	A	C	U	C	A
N	A	O	C	O	T	T	N	P	R	N	T
O	C	A	N	M	A	G	O	T	R	O	I
S	H	I	A	L	R	A	P	M	Z	O	X

Greater Name of Power	Elemental Attribution
OROIBAHAOZPI	Zodiac of Air

King	Elemental Attribution
BATAIVAH	Sol of Air

Seniors	Elemental Attribution
HABIORO	Mars of Air
AAOZAIF	Jupiter of Air
HTMORDA	Mercury of Air
AHAOZPI	Venus of Air
HIPOTGA	Saturn of Air
AVTOTAR	Luna of Air

Air of Air

R	Z	I	L	A
A	R	D	Z	A
C	Z	O	N	S
T	O	I	T	T
S	I	G	A	S
F	M	O	N	D

Wardens	Elemental Attribution
ERZLA	Air of Air
RZLA	(Air of Air) of Air
ZLAR	(Water of Air) of Air
LARZ	(Earth of Air) of Air
ARZL	(Fire of Air) of Air

Masters	Elemental Attribution
IDOIGO & ARDZA	Air of Air
CZNS	(Air of Air) of Air
TOTT	(Water of Air) of Air
SAIS	(Earth of Air) of Air
FMND	(Fire of Air) of Air

Children	Elemental Attribution
OGIODI & AZDRA	Air of Air
XCZ & XNS	(Air of Air) of Air
ATO & ATT	(Water of Air) of Air
RSI & RAS	(Earth of Air) of Air
PFM & PND	(Fire of Air) of Air

Water of Air

Y	T	L	P	A
P	A	L	A	M
O	Y	A	V	B
P	A	C	O	C
R	B	Z	N	H
D	I	A	R	I

Wardens	Elemental Attribution
EYTPA	Water of Air
YTPA	(Air of Water) of Air
TPAY	(Water of Water) of Air
PAYT	(Earth of Water) of Air
AYTP	(Fire of Water) of Air

Masters	Elemental Attribution
LLACZA & PALAM	Water of Air
OYVB	(Air of Water) of Air
PAOC	(Water of Water) of Air
RBNH	(Earth of Water) of Air
DIRI	(Fire of Water) of Air

Children	Elemental Attribution
AZCALL & MALAP	Water of Air
XOY & XVB	(Air of Water) of Air
APA & AOC	(Water of Water) of Air
RRB & RNH	(Earth of Water) of Air
PDI & PRI	(Fire of Water) of Air

Earth of Air

T	N	A	B	R
O	I	I	I	T
A	B	A	M	O
N	A	O	C	O
O	C	A	N	M
S	H	I	A	L

Wardens	Elemental Attribution
ETNBR	Earth of Air
TNBR	(Air of Earth) of Air
NBRT	(Water of Earth) of Air
BRTN	(Earth of Earth) of Air
RTNB	(Fire of Earth) of Air

Masters	Elemental Attribution
AIAOAI & OIIIT	Earth of Air
ABMO	(Air of Earth) of Air
NACO	(Water of Earth) of Air
OCNM	(Earth of Earth) of Air
SHAL	(Fire of Earth) of Air

Children	Elemental Attribution
IAOAIA & TIIIO	Earth of Air
XAB & XMO	(Air of Earth) of Air
ANA & ACO	(Water of Earth) of Air
ROC & RNM	(Earth of Earth) of Air
PSH & PAL	(Fire of Earth) of Air

Fire of Air

X	G	A	S	D
A	L	O	A	I
A	C	U	C	A
N	P	R	N	T
O	T	R	O	I
P	M	Z	O	X

Wardens	Elemental Attribution
EXGSD	Fire of Air
XGSD	(Air of Fire) of Air
GSDX	(Water of Fire) of Air
SDXG	(Earth of Fire) of Air
DXGS	(Fire of Fire) of Air

Masters	Elemental Attribution
AOURRZ & ALOAI	Fire of Air
ACCA	(Air of Fire) of Air
NPNT	(Water of Fire) of Air
OTOI	(Earth of Fire) of Air
PMOX	(Fire of Fire) of Air

Children	Elemental Attribution
ZRRUOA & IAOLA	Fire of Air
XAC & XCA	(Air of Fire) of Air
ANP & ANT	(Water of Fire) of Air
ROT & ROI	(Earth of Fire) of Air
PPM & POX	(Fire of Fire) of Air

WATCHTOWER OF WATER

T	A	O	A	D	V	P	T	D	N	I	M
A	A	B	C	O	O	R	O	M	E	B	B
T	O	G	C	O	N	X	M	A	L	G	M
N	H	O	D	D	I	A	L	E	A	O	C
P	A	T	A	X	I	O	V	S	P	S	N
S	A	A	I	X	A	A	R	V	R	O	I
M	P	H	A	R	S	L	G	A	I	O	L
M	A	M	G	L	O	I	N	L	I	R	X
O	L	A	A	D	N	G	A	T	A	P	A
P	A	L	C	O	I	D	X	P	A	C	N
N	D	A	Z	N	Z	I	V	A	A	S	A
I	I	D	P	O	N	S	D	A	S	P	I
X	R	I	N	H	T	A	R	N	D	I	L

Greater Name of Power	Elemental Attribution
MPHARSLGAIOL	Zodiac of Water

King	Elemental Attribution
RAAGIOSL	Sol of Water

Seniors	Elemental Attribution
LSRAHPM	Mars of Water
SAIINOV	Jupiter of Water
LAOAXRP	Mercury of Water
SLGAIOL	Venus of Water
LIGDISA	Saturn of Water
SONIZNT	Luna of Water

Air of Water

T	A	O	A	D
A	A	B	C	O
T	O	G	C	O
N	H	O	D	D
P	A	T	A	X
S	A	A	I	X

Wardens	Elemental Attribution
HTAAD	Air of Water
TAAD	(Air of Air) of Water
AADT	(Water of Air) of Water
ADTA	(Earth of Air) of Water
DTAA	(Fire of Air) of Water

Masters	Elemental Attribution
OBGOTA & AABCO	Air of Water
TOCO	(Air of Air) of Water
NHDD	(Water of Air) of Water
PAAX	(Earth of Air) of Water
SAIX	(Fire of Air) of Water

Children	Elemental Attribution
ATOGBO & OCBAA	Air of Water
CTO & CCO	(Air of Air) of Water
OHN & ODD	(Water of Air) of Water
MPA & MAX	(Earth of Air) of Water
ASA & AIX	(Fire of Air) of Water

Water of Water

T	D	N	I	M
O	M	E	B	B
M	A	L	G	M
L	E	A	O	C
V	S	P	S	N
R	V	R	O	I

Wardens	Elemental Attribution
HTDIM	Water of Water
TDIM	(Air of Water) of Water
DIMT	(Water of Water) of Water
IMTD	(Earth of Water) of Water
MTDI	(Fire of Water) of Water

Masters	Elemental Attribution
NELAPR & OMEBB	Water of Water
MAGM	(Air of Water) of Water
LEOC	(Water of Water) of Water
VSSN	(Earth of Water) of Water
RVOI	(Fire of Water) of Water

Children	Elemental Attribution
RPALEN & BBEMO	Water of Water
CMA & CGM	(Air of Water) of Water
OLE & OOC	(Water of Water) of Water
MVS & MSN	(Earth of Water) of Water
ARV & AOI	(Fire of Water) of Water

Earth of Water

M	A	M	G	L
O	L	A	A	D
P	A	L	C	O
N	D	A	Z	N
I	I	D	P	O
X	R	I	N	H

Wardens	Elemental Attribution
HMAGL	Earth of Water
MAGL	(Air of Earth) of Water
AGLM	(Water of Earth) of Water
GLMA	(Earth of Earth) of Water
LMAG	(Fire of Earth) of Water

Masters	Elemental Attribution
MALADI & OLAAD	Earth of Water
PACO	(Air of Earth) of Water
NDZN	(Water of Earth) of Water
IIPO	(Earth of Earth) of Water
XRNH	(Fire of Earth) of Water

Children	Elemental Attribution
IDALAM & DAALO	Earth of Water
CPA & CCO	(Air of Earth) of Water
OND & OZN	(Water of Earth) of Water
MII & MPO	(Earth of Earth) of Water
AXR & ANH	(Fire of Earth) of Water

Fire of Water

N	L	I	R	X
A	T	A	P	A
X	P	A	C	N
V	A	A	S	A
D	A	S	P	I
R	N	D	I	L

Wardens	Elemental Attribution
HNLRX	Fire of Water
NLRX	(Air of Fire) of Water
LRXN	(Water of Fire) of Water
RXNL	(Earth of Fire) of Water
XNLR	(Fire of Fire) of Water

Masters	Elemental Attribution
IAAASD & ATAPA	Fire of Water
XPCN	(Air of Fire) of Water
VASA	(Water of Fire) of Water
DAPI	(Earth of Fire) of Water
RNIL	(Fire of Fire) of Water

Children	Elemental Attribution
DSAAAI & APATA	Fire of Water
CXP & CCN	(Air of Fire) of Water
OVA & OSA	(Water of Fire) of Water
MDA & MPI	(Earth of Fire) of Water
ARN & AIL	(Fire of Fire) of Water

WATCHTOWER OF EARTH

B	O	A	Z	A	R	O	P	H	A	R	A
U	N	N	A	X	O	P	S	O	N	D	N
A	I	G	R	A	N	O	O	M	A	G	G
O	R	P	M	N	I	N	G	B	E	A	L
R	S	O	N	I	Z	I	R	L	E	M	V
I	Z	I	N	R	C	Z	I	A	M	H	L
M	O	R	D	I	A	L	H	C	T	G	A
O	C	A	N	C	H	I	A	S	O	M	T
A	R	B	I	Z	M	I	I	L	P	I	Z
O	P	A	N	A	L	A	M	S	M	A	P
D	O	L	O	P	I	N	I	A	N	B	A
R	X	P	A	O	C	S	I	Z	I	X	P
A	X	T	I	R	V	A	S	T	R	I	M

Greater Name of Power	Elemental Attribution
MORDIALHCTGA	Zodiac of Earth

King	Elemental Attribution
ICZHIHAL	Sol of Earth

Seniors	Elemental Attribution
LAIDROM	Mars of Earth
ACZINOR	Jupiter of Earth
LZINOPO	Mercury of Earth
ALHCTGA	Venus of Earth
LIIANSA	Saturn of Earth
AHMLICV	Luna of Earth

Air of Earth

B	O	A	Z	A
U	N	N	A	X
A	I	G	R	A
O	R	P	M	N
R	S	O	N	I
I	Z	I	N	R

Wardens	Elemental Attribution
NBOZA	Air of Earth
BOZA	(Air of Air) of Earth
OZAB	(Water of Air) of Earth
ZABO	(Earth of Air) of Earth
ABOZ	(Fire of Air) of Earth

Masters	Elemental Attribution
ANGPOI & UNNAX	Air of Earth
AIRA	(Air of Air) of Earth
ORMN	(Water of Air) of Earth
RSNI	(Earth of Air) of Earth
IZNR	(Fire of Air) of Earth

Children	Elemental Attribution
IOPGNA & XANNU	Air of Earth
AAI & ARA	(Air of Air) of Earth
NOR & NMN	(Water of Air) of Earth
TRS & TNI	(Earth of Air) of Earth
AIZ & ANR	(Fire of Air) of Earth

Water of Earth

P	H	A	R	A
S	O	N	D	N
O	M	A	G	G
G	B	E	A	L
R	L	E	M	V
I	A	M	H	L

Wardens	Elemental Attribution
NPHRA	Water of Earth
PHRA	(Air of Water) of Earth
HRAP	(Water of Water) of Earth
RAPH	(Earth of Water) of Earth
APHR	(Fire of Water) of Earth

Masters	Elemental Attribution
ANAEEM & SONDN	Water of Earth
OMGG	(Air of Water) of Earth
GBAL	(Water of Water) of Earth
RLMV	(Earth of Water) of Earth
IAHL	(Fire of Water) of Earth

Children	Elemental Attribution
MEEANA & NDNOS	Water of Earth
AOM & AGG	(Air of Water) of Earth
NGB & NAL	(Water of Water) of Earth
TRL & TMV	(Earth of Water) of Earth
AIA & AHL	(Fire of Water) of Earth

Earth of Earth

O	C	A	N	C
A	R	B	I	Z
O	P	A	N	A
D	O	L	O	P
R	X	P	A	O
A	X	T	I	R

Wardens	Elemental Attribution
NOCNC	Earth of Earth
OCNC	(Air of Earth) of Earth
CNCO	(Water of Earth) of Earth
NCOC	(Earth of Earth) of Earth
COCN	(Fire of Earth) of Earth

Masters	Elemental Attribution
ABALPT & ARBIZ	Earth of Earth
OPNA	(Air of Earth) of Earth
DOOP	(Water of Earth) of Earth
RXAO	(Earth of Earth) of Earth
AXIR	(Fire of Earth) of Earth

Children	Elemental Attribution
TPLABA & ZIBRA	Earth of Earth
AOP & ANA	(Air of Earth) of Earth
NDO & NOP	(Water of Earth) of Earth
TRX & TAO	(Earth of Earth) of Earth
AAX & AIR	(Fire of Earth) of Earth

Fire of Earth

A	S	O	M	T
I	L	P	I	Z
M	S	M	A	P
I	A	N	B	A
I	Z	I	X	P
S	T	R	I	M

Wardens	Elemental Attribution
NASMT	Fire of Earth
ASMT	(Air of Fire) of Earth
SMTA`	(Water of Fire) of Earth
MTAS	(Earth of Fire) of Earth
TASM	(Fire of Fire) of Earth

Masters	Elemental Attribution
OPMNIR & ILPIZ	Fire of Earth
MSAP	(Air of Fire) of Earth
IABA	(Water of Fire) of Earth
IZXP	(Earth of Fire) of Earth
STIM	(Fire of Fire) of Earth

Children	Elemental Attribution
RINMPO & ZIPLI	Fire of Earth
AMS & AAP	(Air of Fire) of Earth
NIA & NBA	(Water of Fire) of Earth
TIZ & TXP	(Earth of Fire) of Earth
AST & AIM	(Fire of Fire) of Earth

WATCHTOWER OF FIRE

D	O	N	P	A	T	D	A	N	V	A	A
O	L	O	A	G	E	O	O	B	A	U	A
O	P	A	M	N	O	V	G	M	D	N	M
A	P	L	S	T	E	D	E	C	A	O	P
S	C	M	I	O	O	N	A	M	L	O	X
V	A	R	S	G	D	L	B	R	I	A	P
O	I	P	T	E	A	A	P	D	O	C	E
P	S	U	A	C	N	R	Z	I	R	Z	A
S	I	O	D	A	O	I	N	R	Z	F	M
D	A	L	T	T	D	N	A	D	I	R	E
D	I	X	O	M	O	N	S	I	O	S	P
O	O	D	P	Z	I	A	P	A	N	L	I
R	G	O	A	N	N	P	A	C	R	A	R

Greater Name of Power	Elemental Attribution
OIPTEAAPDOCE	Zodiac of Fire

King	Elemental Attribution
EDLPRNAA	Sol of Fire

Seniors	Elemental Attribution
AAETPIO	Mars of Fire
ADOEOET	Jupiter of Fire
ALNDVOD	Mercury of Fire
AAPDOCE	Venus of Fire
ARINNAP	Saturn of Fire
ANODOIN	Luna of Fire

Air of Fire

D	O	N	P	A
O	L	O	A	G
O	P	A	M	N
A	P	L	S	T
S	C	M	I	O
V	A	R	S	G

Wardens	Elemental Attribution
BDOPA	Air of Fire
DOPA	(Air of Air) of Fire
OPAD	(Water of Air) of Fire
PADO	(Earth of Air) of Fire
ADOP	(Fire of Air) of Fire

Masters	Elemental Attribution
NOALMR & OLOAG	Air of Fire
OPMN	(Air of Air) of Fire
APST	(Water of Air) of Fire
SCIO	(Earth of Air) of Fire
VASG	(Fire of Air) of Fire

Children	Elemental Attribution
RMLAON & GAOLO	Air of Fire
IOP & IMN	(Air of Air) of Fire
TAP & TST	(Water of Air) of Fire
OSC & OIO	(Earth of Air) of Fire
MVA & VSG	(Fire of Air) of Fire

Water of Fire

A	N	V	A	A
O	B	A	U	A
G	M	D	N	M
E	C	A	O	P
A	M	L	O	X
B	R	I	A	P

Wardens	Elemental Attribution
BANAA	Water of Fire
ANAA	(Air of Water) of Fire
NAAA	(Water of Water) of Fire
AAAN	(Earth of Water) of Fire
AANA	(Fire of Water) of Fire

Masters	Elemental Attribution
VADALI & OBAUA	Water of Fire
GMNM	(Air of Water) of Fire
ECOP	(Water of Water) of Fire
AMOX	(Earth of Water) of Fire
BRAP	(Fire of Water) of Fire

Children	Elemental Attribution
ILADAV & AUABO	Water of Fire
IGM & INM	(Air of Water) of Fire
TEC & TOP	(Water of Water) of Fire
OAM & OOX	(Earth of Water) of Fire
MBR & MAP	(Fire of Water) of Fire

Earth of Fire

P	S	U	A	C
S	I	O	D	A
D	A	L	T	T
D	I	X	O	M
O	O	D	P	Z
R	G	O	A	N

Wardens	Elemental Attribution
BPSAC	Earth of Fire
PSAC	(Air of Earth) of Fire
SACP	(Water of Earth) of Fire
ACPS	(Earth of Earth) of Fire
CPSA	(Fire of Earth) of Fire

Masters	Elemental Attribution
UOLXDO & SIODA	Earth of Fire
DATT	(Air of Earth) of Fire
DIOM	(Water of Earth) of Fire
OOPZ	(Earth of Earth) of Fire
RGAN	(Fire of Earth) of Fire

Children	Elemental Attribution
ODXLOU & ADOIS	Earth of Fire
IDA & ITT	(Air of Earth) of Fire
TDI & TOM	(Water of Earth) of Fire
OOO & OPZ	(Earth of Earth) of Fire
MRG & MAN	(Fire of Earth) of Fire

10

Fire of Fire

Z	I	R	Z	A
N	R	Z	F	M
A	D	I	R	E
S	I	O	S	P
P	A	N	L	I
A	C	R	A	R

Wardens	Elemental Attribution
BZIZA	Fire of Fire
ZIZA	(Air of Fire) of Fire
IZAZ	(Water of Fire) of Fire
ZAZI	(Earth of Fire) of Fire
AZIZ	(Fire of Fire) of Fire

Masters	Elemental Attribution
RZIONR & NRZFM	Fire of Fire
ADRE	(Air of Fire) of Fire
SISP	(Water of Fire) of Fire
PALI	(Earth of Fire) of Fire
ACAR	(Fire of Fire) of Fire

Children	Elemental Attribution
RNOIZR & MFZRN	Fire of Fire
IAD & IRE	(Air of Fire) of Fire
TSI & TSP	(Water of Fire) of Fire
OPA & OLI	(Earth of Fire) of Fire
MAC & MAR	(Fire of Fire) of Fire

BIBLIOGRAPHY

Bardon, Franz. *The Practice of Magical Evocation.* West Germany: Dieter Rüggeberg/Wuppertal, 1975.

Black, S. Jason and Christopher S. Hyatt. *Pacts with the Devil.* Tempe, AZ: New Falcon, 1997.

Carroll, Peter J. *Liber Null & Psychonaut.* York Beach, ME: Samuel Weiser, 1987.

Cicero, Chic and Sandra Tabatha Cicero. *Self-Initiation into the Golden Dawn Tradition.* St. Paul, MN: Llewellyn, 1995.

Cortens, Theolyn. *Working with Archangels: A Path to Transformation and Power.* London: Piatkus Books, 2007.

Crowley, Aleister. *Magick (Book 4, Parts I -IV).* Hymenaeus Beta, ed. York Beach, ME: Samuel Weiser, 2000.
—*Magick Without Tears.* Tempe, AZ: New Falcon, 1994

Crowley, Aleister, ed. *The Goetia: The Lesser Key of Solomon the King.* S.L. MacGregor Mathers, tr. York Beach, ME: Samuel Weiser, 1995.

Davidson, Gustav . *A Dictionary of Angels, Including the Fallen Angels.* London: The Free Press, 1967.

Denning, Melita and Osborne Phillips. *Mysteria Magica: The Magical Philosophy Vol.3.* St. Paul, MN: Llewellyn, 1988.

DuQuette, Lon Milo. *Angels, Demons & Gods of the New Millennium.* York Beach, ME: Samuel Weiser, 1997.
—*My Life with the Spirits.* York Beach, ME: Samuel Weiser, 1999.
—*Tarot of Ceremonial Magick.* York Beach, ME: Samuel Weiser, 1995.

DuQuette, Lon Milo, and Christopher S. Hyatt. *Enochian World of Aleister Crowley*. Tempe, AZ: New Falcon, 1997.

Dukes, Ramsey. *Uncle Ramsey's Little Book of Demons*. London: Aeon, 2005.

Hamilton, Edith. *Mythology*. Boston, MA: Little, Brown and Company, 1998.

James, Geoffery. *Angel Magic*. St. Paul, MN: Llewellyn, 1995.
—*The Enochian Magick of Dr. John Dee*. St. Paul, MN: Llewellyn, 1994.

Konstantinos. *Summoning Spirits*. St. Paul, MN: Llewellyn, 2004.

Kraig, Donald Michael. *Modern Magick*. Woodbury, MN: Llewellyn, 2010.

LaVey, Anton Szandor. *The Satanic Bible*. New York: Avon, 1969.

Laycock, Donald C. *The Complete Enochian Dictionary*. York Beach, ME: Samuel Weiser, 1994.

Leitch, Aaron. *The Angelical Language*, vols. 1 & 2. St. Paul, MN: Llewellyn, 2010.
—*Secrets of the Magickal Grimoires*. Woodbury, MN: Llewellyn, 2005.

Lovelock, James. *The Ages of Gaia*. rev.ed. New York: W.W. Norton, 1995.

Mathers, Samuel Liddel MacGregor, ed. & tr. *The Key of Solomon the King*. York Beach, ME: Samuel Weiser, 1984.

Open Source Order of the Golden Dawn. www.osogd.org

Peterson, Joseph, ed. *The Lesser Key of Solomon*. York Beach, ME: Weiser Books, 2001.

Regardie, Israel. *The Golden Dawn*, 6th ed. St. Paul, MN: Llewellyn, 1994.

Rowe, Benjamin. *Godzilla Meets E.T., Parts 1 & 2.* (1994). Available at www.hermetic.com.

Savedow, Steve. *Goetic Evocation.* Chicago: Eschaton, 1996.

Skinner, Stephen and David Rankine. *The Goetia of Dr. Rudd.* London: Golden Hoard, 2007.

Snuffin, Michael Osiris. *The Thoth Companion.* Woodbury, MN: Llewellyn, 2007.

Turner, Robert. *Elizabethan Magick.* Shaftesbury: Element Books, 1989.

Zalewski, Pat. *Golden Dawn Enochian Magic.* St. Paul, MN: Llewellyn, 1994.

ABOUT THE AUTHOR

Michael Osiris Snuffin has studied and practiced various forms of occultism for almost twenty-five years, with particular interest in the Golden Dawn, Thelema, Chaos Magick and the Left-Hand Path. Michael has published two books: *The Thoth Companion* (Llewellyn Publications, 2007), an in-depth analysis of the symbolism in Aleister Crowley's Thoth tarot; and *Introduction to Romantic Satanism* (Throned Eye Press, 2020), an overview of the 19th century artistic and political movement that recast Satan as a heroic rebel in a struggle against oppression and injustice. He has given lectures and written essays on Thelema, evocation, tarot, and other occult subjects, and has published some of his work at **www.hermetic.com/Osiris.**

Michael Osiris Snuffin has a BA in Liberal Arts with an emphasis in Communications and Media from The Evergreen State College, and has earned a Certificate in Editing from the University of Washington. He lives in Tacoma, Washington, where he works as a freelance non-fiction book editor and author.

· · · *A Note on Design* · · ·

Book design and inking by Lena Kartzov.

Main body typeface and subheads are Centaur family.
Tables typeface is Trebuchet, and headline script
is Signatra by Fontdation. Printing by Kindle.

All symbols were custom drawn for this book with
fountain pen and ink on paper by candle light.

· · ·

Made in USA - Kendallville, IN
1209756_9798625917827
01.19.2021 1817